The Meaning of Church Membership

The Meaning of Church Membership

by
Jerry W. McCant

Beacon Hill Press of Kansas City
Kansas City, Missouri

First Printing, 1973

Printed in the United States of America

Acknowledgment is made of permission granted to quote from the following copyrighted versions of the Bible:

The Living Bible (paraphrased), by Kenneth N. Taylor, © 1971 by Tyndale House Publishers, Wheaton, Ill. (LB)

The Revised Standard Version of the Holy Bible, copyright 1946, 1952 by the Division of Christian Education of the National Council of Churches. (RSV)

The Bible: A New Translation, by James Moffatt. Copyright 1950, 1952, 1953, 1954 by James A. R. Moffatt. Used by permission of Harper and Row.

The New Testament in Modern English, © J. B. Phillips, 1958. Used by permission of the Macmillan Co.

The New English Bible, © The Delegates of the Oxford University Press and the Syndics of the Cambridge University Press, 1961. (NEB)

Contents

Preface 7
1. Things Are Different Now! 9
2. The Church of Jesus Christ 21
3. Meet the Nazarenes 40
4. A Church in the Making 62
5. An International Church 79
6. Beliefs and Standards 99
Reference Notes 118

Preface

They were powerful words! Those words of Jesus: "I will build my church" (Matt. 16:18)! That the Church does belong to Christ is one of the easiest things for church people to forget. It is His Church from start to finish. And He is right—"The gates of hell shall not prevail against it." It is His body and He will take care of His Church.

Every believer belongs to Christ's Church. Belonging to the one true Church is more important than membership in any denomination. To belong to Christ means to belong to His Church. It is to be a part of the great body of Jesus Christ. This is the Church that is to be without "spot, or wrinkle" and having no "blemish" when He comes back to earth again.

A deep appreciation for the body of Christ should not lessen one's appreciation for his particular denomination. I am a Nazarene by choice and am pleased to be a part of such a great denomination. The church of my choice is certainly a part of the body of Christ. In it I have found not only salvation, but a place to serve God in the field of labor to which He has called me.

This manuscript has been prepared with a deep sense of my own inadequacy. It is my prayer that it will prove half the blessing to the reader that it has been to me as I worked in preparing it. I pray that every new Nazarene who reads it will feel a deep love and appreciation for his church. That is the love I feel for my church and would have every other Nazarene feel.

—Jerry W. McCant

Instructions for Receiving
Christian Service Training Credit

1. This is the text for First Series Unit 132a, "The Meaning of Church Membership." Six 50-minute sessions, or the equivalent in time, are required.
2. Your class should be registered with the CST office at least three weeks before your first class session. This will allow time for the office to get the class report forms and individual registration slips to you.
3. Each pupil must be present for five of the six sessions to receive credit.
4. Examinations are optional with the teacher.
5. For Home Study purposes a Study Guide is available, and credit is granted when written work has been sent to the general office.

CHRISTIAN SERVICE TRAINING
6401 The Paseo
Kansas City, Mo. 64131

Chapter 1

Things Are Different Now!

So, you are a Christian! You are literally bursting with joy. And why not? The greatest thing *ever* has happened to you. Joy-bells are ringing in your heart. Your first impulse is to shout at the top of your voice, "Jesus really does save!" All the world looks different—and it is! There's a song in your soul that won't keep quiet. You have a reason to sing!

Nothing so wonderful and exciting has ever happened to you before. God has brought new life to you. Go down the list and check them off. Your first date can't compare to this. Learning to drive in no way parallels conversion. Buying your first car was not as exciting. Even your wedding day was not so thrilling. This is the greatest thing that has ever happened in your life.

Could you explain what has happened to you? Probably not. Most likely, you have felt little or no need to explain it. After all, how could anyone ever explain it anyway? Maybe you feel like the blind man Jesus healed. He could not explain how Jesus healed him to the satisfaction of the Pharisees. His testimony, however, was a real clincher. He said, "One thing I know, that, whereas I was blind, now I see" (John 9:25).

And so you say, "All I really know is that Jesus saved me!" That is enough to satisfy you now. Peter, of course, would remind you to "be ready always to give an answer to every man that asketh you a reason of the hope that is in you" (I Pet. 3:15). This means you need to be able to understand and intelligently discuss what has happened to you.

Let's spend some time together trying now to understand what has taken place in your life. The "reason of the hope" is not essential to your salvation. You can certainly be saved without understanding fully the theology of conversion. When you try to lead another person to Christ, however, it does become necessary. God wants us to be intelligent Christians. He wants to come into our minds as well as our hearts!

How It Got Started

Who is responsible for your being a Christian? Take time to think before you answer. Are you ready now? Did you come up with more than one name? If so, don't worry, because that is normal. Undoubtedly many people influenced your decision to receive Christ as Saviour. Pinning the credit for your conversion on a single person is not really important. Paul said he could not claim that he was solely responsible for anyone's conversion. This is the way he put it: "I have planted, Apollos watered, but God gave the increase" (I Cor. 3:6). Just give God all the credit, glory, and praise. If you do, you will never go wrong. After all, salvation is "the gift of God" (Eph. 2:8).

Somewhere a gospel seed was planted in your heart by

someone. As it happened, the soil of your heart was "good soil" (Matt. 13:3-8). Your heart was receptive and the soil was fertile. By faith and through grace you responded positively to the seeking love of God. As a healthy Christian you are now producing Christian fruits. Jesus said some produced at thirtyfold; others at sixtyfold; still others at a hundredfold level of productivity.

THE HOLY SPIRIT AND YOUR CONVERSION

According to John 16:8, one of the chief activities of the Holy Spirit is convicting people of sin. Everyone who comes to Jesus feels this to a greater or lesser degree. Christians pray that the Holy Spirit will "convict" others of sin. Do you remember when your sense of guilt weighed you down? Conviction is when all the sins of your life stare you in the face and accuse you. Nothing in your life will ever make you feel more miserable. There is no heavier load than a guilty conscience.

Conviction is that extreme sense of guilt when one recognizes that he is a sinner before God. The Holy Spirit exposes our sins to us. He lifts the blindness Satan has put on our eyes. Sin is brought to the attention of the conscience and the conscience is awakened. To convict means to prove guilty on the basis of the evidence. When the Holy Spirit brings in the evidence, all we can do is plead, "Guilty."

David was experiencing this very thing when he cried, "My sin is ever before me" (Ps. 51:1). There is no hiding place, nowhere to run. No preacher need point an accusing finger at a guilty conscience; the conscience furnishes one of its own! Out of such desperation, you no doubt cried to God for forgiveness and salvation.

A psychiatrist once said: "A man can live with social deprivation and excruciating pain, but he cannot long live with a guilty conscience." Isaiah described his feeling of conviction as being "unclean" (Isa. 6:5). Thank God that He not only convicts of sin, but can deliver from sin and its guilt.

There must come the sense of total inadequacy in the face of sin. Spiritual bankruptcy papers must be filed with heaven before you can know the joy of sins forgiven. In Romans 7, Paul declares himself unable to break the chains of sin and go free. With the sigh of resignation he prays, "O wretched man that I am! who shall deliver me from the body of this death?" (Rom. 7:24) Now you, like Paul, came to say, "I thank God through Jesus Christ our Lord. . . . There is therefore now no condemnation to them which are in Christ Jesus" (Rom. 7:26—8:1).

God's Forgiveness

Strangely enough, accepting God's forgiveness is hard for many people. Most of us cannot believe it is possible. Usually it is hard for us to forgive, and as a result we find it difficult to believe that God forgives. But God's word is so clear, "While we were yet sinners, Christ died for us" (Rom. 5:8). And the Psalmist declares, "He has removed our sins as far away from us as the east is from the west" (Ps. 103:12, LB). Micah says, "Thou wilt cast our sins in the depths of the sea" (7:19). God assures us, "Their sins . . . will I remember no more" (Heb. 10:17).

Take God at His word! Don't allow the specter of your sins to terrify you. There is no need to suffer the pains of guilt any longer. You are forgiven now—this very moment. You need wait no longer; penance is not necessary for forgiveness.

A lady was having trouble exercising faith for salvation. She pleaded, "Pastor, the Lord will forgive if I keep praying hard enough, won't He?" It was this writer's happy privilege to remind her God had already forgiven her. Through tears the words tumbled out, "You mean He has *already* forgiven and I don't need to keep begging Him?" Assured that this was the case, she rejoiced, and added, "This is almost as good as getting saved!" It *was* "getting saved."

Facing Temptation

Now that you are saved, you must live the Christian life. Unfortunately, living that life includes facing temptations. Unintentionally, ministers too frequently leave the impression that conversion ends the spiritual struggle. When people, however, take a definite stand for God, Satan then tries his worst to upset them. No state of grace and no amount of growing in grace grants exemption from temptation. Nor does age or saintliness deliver one from the pesky problem.

Satan tempts us through our normal, human, God-given desires. It is through our "desires" (Jas. 1:14, RSV) that he gets to us. Sometimes guilt prevents our admitting there is any real desire to do wrong. Unless there is desire, however, temptation is an utter impossibility. None of our human desires and drives in themselves are sinful. Rather, they are necessary to our humanity and well-being. Yet it is through these very avenues that the devil tempts us.

Temptation is progressive in nature. First, desire is aroused (Jas. 1:14). Then the will is attacked. It is only then that the matter becomes a moral question. There is real struggle in the citadel of the soul. The first question is whether it is right or wrong. When that is established, it becomes a matter of whether or not to do it. Working hard on the will, Satan will try to get one to do the wrong thing. Failing that, he may try to convince you that desire is as bad as the act. That's one of his biggest lies! Don't let the enemy destroy you with guilt over temptation. Too many backslide at precisely this point.

You now stand at the crossroads and a decision is imperative. Temptation cannot remain temptation. Either it becomes sin or a victory. You decide which it becomes! Sin enters only when the will gives consent and yields. Resist the devil's first advance. If we will be sensitive to the leadership of the Holy Spirit, He will be faithful to warn and strengthen us.

Oscar Wilde is reported to have said, "I can resist everything except temptation." He concludes, "The only way to get rid of temptation is to yield to it." That represents the philosophy of sinful, defeated man—not the Christian philosophy! It is true that we cannot escape temptation. But, thanks be to God, we can be overcomers. Prayer, God's Word, and the power of the indwelling Holy Spirit make it possible. Give your temptation to God; the battle is the Lord's—not yours!

Jesus told an eerie little story of the empty, haunted house. It is recorded in Luke 11:24-26 and Matt. 12:43-45. A demon was driven from the house and went into the desert. Finding no pleasure there, he said, "I will return to my house." Upon return he found the house, clean, swept, garnished [well-furnished], but *empty*. Immediately he and seven other evil spirits moved in!

You can mark it down as an inexorable law—the devil always comes back. He feels rather possessive of you and wants to return to "my house." He never gives up. Peering in through the windows, he tries to learn what activity has taken place. With haste he plants doubts in your mind. Jesus suffered the same struggle as the adversary said, "If thou be the Son of God . . ." Never once did that fallen angel give up. As Jesus died on Calvary, one of Satan's representatives located on another cross cried, *"If* thou be the Son of God . . ."

Satan's goal is to make you doubt that Jesus saved you. He will destroy you with that doubt—if he can. The advice

James gives us is, "Resist the devil, and he will flee from you" (4:7). "Resist" means "stand up to"; so stand up to the devil and he will hightail it out of sight!

Whatever you do, don't let Satan come back and find an empty house. You cannot keep him from returning but you don't have to keep an empty house. If the house is empty, he will move back in. Fill your life with God and holiness. Get busy and involved in service to God. When your house is filled with Christ, there is no room for him to get back in. With a full house, you can just hang a "No Vacancy" sign on your door!

You Need to Be Sanctified

Upon his arrival at Ephesus, Paul asked a disturbing question. It was this: "Have ye received the Holy Ghost since ye believed?" (Acts 19:2) The answer was an unqualified "No." Paul immediately prayed for them to receive the Holy Spirit.

Entire sanctification and the baptism of the Holy Spirit are one and the same experience. Jesus prayed for His disciples to be sanctified (John 17). If this did not take place on the Day of Pentecost, we have no record that Jesus' great high-priestly prayer was ever answered. Acts 15:8-9 is the clearest possible evidence that it is through the baptism of the Holy Spirit that the heart is "cleansed"—sanctified.

A second definite work of grace is needed. The disciples who had walked with Jesus were commanded, "Tarry ye in the city of Jerusalem, until ye be endued with power from on high" (Luke 24:49). They indeed did tarry and were filled with the Holy Spirit (Acts 2). Even John the Baptist saw this need. He said you needed a baptism of water—repentance—and a baptism with the Holy Spirit and fire (Matt. 3:11). It has already been noted that at Ephesus they needed a second touch from God.

Don't settle down where you are. If you have not already been sanctified, start praying to that end today. The writer of the Hebrews admonishes, "Go on unto perfection" (Heb. 6:1). And again he reminds us that without holiness "no man shall see the Lord" (12:14). Holiness of heart and life is the answer to an up-and-down, vacillating experience. Paul's prayer for you is that God will "establish your hearts unblamable in holiness" (I Thess. 3:13, RSV).

Sanctification is no sideline doctrine. It is an aspect of our doctrine of atonement. When we talk about holiness we are talking about full salvation. This is not optional equipment, like air conditioning or power brakes on your car! Sanctification is God's will for you (I Thess. 4:3). He has called all men to holiness (I Thess. 4:7).

There is nothing static about holiness. It is a moving, ongoing experience. Holiness begins as an initial experience in regeneration. This is often referred to as "initial sanctification." In no sense should this be understood to suggest that you simply grow or expand on your new life in Christ until you are sanctified. Regeneration and sanctification are two distinct works of grace. However, as H. Orton Wiley points out, "This new life, being one of 'holy love,' may be said to be the beginning of holiness."[1]

Entire sanctification (holiness) is a crisis experience. It is a "dateable event" in one's life. We refer to the "Day of Pentecost," not the "year of Pentecost." At Ephesus, Paul laid hands on the disciples and they received the Holy Spirit (Acts 19:6). Philip conducted a great revival in Samaria and many turned to the Lord. Peter and John, acting for all the disciples, went and prayed for these believers and they received the Holy Spirit (Acts 8:14-17). Ananias came to see the new convert, Saul, saying, "Brother Saul, the Lord Jesus . . . has sent me that you may regain your sight and be filled with the Holy Spirit" (Acts 9:17, RSV).

Holiness is also a progressive experience. We must pursue and keep on pursuing holiness (Heb. 12:14). Only God is holy in the absolute sense. We must ever be seeking to become more like Him who is perfectly holy. Never cease to pray:

> *Oh, to be like Thee! Oh, to be like Thee,*
> *Blessed Redeemer, pure as Thou art!*
> *Come in Thy sweetness, come in Thy fullness;*
> *Stamp Thine own image deep on my heart.*
> —T. O. CHISHOLM

Sanctification is instantaneous *and* progressive. "If we walk in the light, as he is in the light, we have fellowship one with another, and the blood of Jesus Christ his Son cleanseth [keeps cleansing] us from all sin" (I John 1:7).

BABIES NEED TO GROW!

A cuddly baby is wonderful—when he's a baby! But when he reaches 40 we don't expect him to still be a cuddly baby. We must advance or retreat as Christians. Either we will grow or we will die. There is no such thing as standing still! Sound advice is, "Grow in grace, and in the knowledge of our Lord and Saviour Jesus Christ" (II Pet. 3:18).

This is only a start; life for you has just begun! The best is yet to be. Don't let your enthusiasm and joy in the Lord die. As Paul put it: "Maintain the spiritual glow" (Rom. 12:11, Moffatt). The secret to keeping this glow in one's experience is through life in the Spirit. As the Christian lives in the power and presence of the Holy Spirit, the newness need not wear off.

Hazen G. Werner has a book entitled *No Saints Suddenly*. That title speaks volumes! Did you ever hear of a baby being born five years old? Neither are Christians born with full maturity. We begin as infants—"newborn babes" (I Pet. 2:2). There are no ready-made saints. All the "babies" must have time to grow.

Babies are born with feet and legs, but they don't start running the first day they are born. They come equipped with tongues, but they do not immediately speak intelligible words. As a "new babe in Christ," expect the same. The first steps of learning to walk will be faltering, stumbling steps. Your first words of prayer may remind you of the baby's first "Da-Da!" But those first steps and words are a thrill to the heart of God. Keep it up! Don't worry and chafe over the fact that someone else is more mature than you. Give yourself time and keep on growing!

Proper growth requires a balanced diet. When you have tasted God's goodness and salvation, "Cry for this as a baby cries for his milk" (I Pet. 2:2, LB). But we must also go beyond the "milk" stage to the "meat" of the Word, if we would grow strong in the Lord (cf. I Cor. 3:2; Heb. 5:12).

Feast your mind on devotional literature. Read the *Herald of Holiness* and *Come Ye Apart;* daily devotional books such as *Truth for Today,* by Bertha Munro; *Every Day with the Psalms,* by Mendell Taylor; and *Holiness and High Country,* by A. F. Harper—and other literature that will build your faith. But don't forget to include some "meaty" books that will make you think hard and long. Be a strong, intelligent Christian. As you grow in grace, be well assured that "he which hath begun a good work in you will perform it until the day of Jesus Christ" (Phil. 1:6).

GET A MOVE ON YOU!

Christianity wears overalls! Its Founder declared that He "came not to be served but to serve" (Mark 10:45, RSV). Peter was so thrilled with his experience on the Mount of Transfiguration that he wanted to stay there. But Jesus took him to the foot of the mountain to look upon human need. That day his service was healing a sick boy. You need not lose the thrill of your mountaintop experience, but you must come down from your ecstatic state to serve others. Many are still crying and thirsting for what you have found.

By no stretch of the imagination can one ever hope to be saved by his good works. But we are saved "unto good works" (Eph. 2:10). After we are saved, we must go to work. There is no place in God's kingdom for loafers! Our service may vary from mowing the church lawn to performing delicate surgery in a mission hospital. Whatever our service, it is holy unto God. He who came to serve also calls you into service.

Don't wait for the pastor to ask you or for the board to appoint you! The most important jobs are not appointive tasks. You can witness, visit, and encourage others without the church board's permission. So plunge in right now and get started. You may need to use your car to bring some children to Sunday school. This might mean getting sufficient and proper clothing for them so they can come. Your task may be caring for some older person who needs love and encouragement. Maybe it will be leading some of society's "unlovables" to the love of God. Get to work, *now!*

Perhaps you are needed to teach a class in Sunday school. Really you want to do it but you don't think you know how. The Sunday school superintendent and pastor have said they need you. What will you do? The best answer is: Train for service. Of course, you cannot take time to go to college to learn to be a Sunday school teacher! But the Church of the Nazarene has made it simpler than that. You can train in your church or home through Christian Service Training. Ask your pastor or CST director about it today.

God has given you a job. No one else can do it and satisfy your obligation before the Lord. Whatever your talents and abilities, use them for God. You are needed in God's work and you dare not shirk your responsibility. Annie Johnson Flint has said it so well:

> *Christ has no hands but our hands*
> *To do His work today;*
> *He has no feet but our feet*
> *To lead men in His way;*
> *He has no tongues but our tongues*
> *To tell men how he died;*
> *He has no help but our help*
> *To bring them to His side.*

Yes, things are different now! You are a "new creature" (II Cor. 5:17). Everything is different for you. In a moment of time, God has cleansed away your sins and they remain buried in the depths of the sea. With this tremendous, earthshaking experience you have begun a process of growth that will last throughout a thrilling lifetime. God is not finished with you yet. He will continue making and shaping you into His perfect image. As someone has put it:

> *I'm a person God is making,*
> *Like a statue God is shaping.*
> *God is changing me, correcting;*
> *God's intent on my perfecting.*

For Your Consideration

1. Why is conviction for sin essential to one's conversion?

2. In your own words explain the difference between being tempted and doing wrong.

3. What is meant by the statement that regeneration is often referred to as "initial sanctification"?

4. How important is growth in grace beyond the crisis experience of entire sanctification?

5. What devotional literature have you found helpful in nourishing your spiritual life?

6. What place do "good works" have in the Christian life?

Chapter 2

The Church of Jesus Christ

How we need a deeper appreciation for the Church of Jesus Christ today! God brought the Church into existence as a means of bringing men to himself. Without this sacred institution, how many of us would be saved? It is through the Church that the work of Christ is continued in the world. This is clearly implied in Acts 1:1. All who profess to be Christians should demonstrate that fact by love for and loyalty to the Church.

Denominationalism may easily overshadow the true meaning of the body of Christ. To overemphasize the importance of one branch of the Church is detrimental to the whole. Regardless of denominational affiliation, all Christians belong to Christ. Likewise, all who have come to Christ through true repentance are members of His Church. In His Church one will find Methodists, Baptists, Lutherans, Nazarenes, and so forth. His body is too inclusive to be contained in any one communion of believers!

In reciting the Apostles' Creed we declare that "we believe in the holy Church of Jesus Christ." (The early form read, "the holy catholic Church," which means "the Church universal"—His Church.) It is the one institution that includes in its creed a statement of belief in itself. Along with such belief is a need for understanding and appreciation. Knowledge always precedes appreciation. A better understanding of the true nature of the Church will bring with it a proper appreciation. Realizing that Christ purchased the Church with His own blood should deepen our love for it. The aim of this chapter is to give that better understanding that will result in a deeper appreciation for the Church.

THE CHURCH'S FOUNDER

Five of the most powerful words ever spoken are, "I will build my church" (Matt. 16:18). Remembering who spoke those tremendous words, they take on new meaning. This declaration of intention followed Peter's great confession, "Thou art the Christ, the Son of the living God" (Matt. 16:16). No theology could ever plumb the depth of meaning in that scene and the words spoken by the Lord at Caesarea Philippi.

Although the Church is composed of redeemed human beings, let it never be forgotten that it is a divine organism. Its Founder and Foundation are divine. No mere human could have ever brought such an institution into existence. Without Christ, there is no Church. It would be hard to express it better than Samuel J. Stone did when he wrote:

> *The Church's one Foundation*
>   *Is Jesus Christ, her Lord.*
> *She is His new creation*
>   *By water and the word.*
> *From heav'n He came and sought her*
>   *To be His holy bride;*
> *With His own blood He bought her,*
>   *And for her life He died.*

Though despised and rejected, He became the "chief corner stone" (I Pet. 2:6). Well in advance of His coming, this rejection was prophesied in Ps. 118:22.

Much discussion has surrounded the "rock" on which Christ said He would build His Church (Matt. 16:18). There is no basis at all for the papacy in this statement. In no way does this make Peter the first pope, nor does it give him any priority as a disciple. Neither Peter nor the other disciples were "foundation" materials. Nothing so unstable and undependable as they would ever serve as a foundation. Had they been the foundation, the Church would have died in the first century! No, Christ is both Founder and Foundation.

There are those (even some far-out churchmen) who say there is no need for the institutional Church today. Some refer to her as a vestige of the past. For a world "come of age," they say, the Church has no significance or meaning. Such claims ignore the fact that basically humanity has not changed. Science and technology have not altered man's basic needs. One may hate his wife just as much while traveling 600 miles per hour as he does when traveling six miles per hour. A man's heart may be just as broken while driving a Cadillac as while driving a horse and buggy. Sickness and trouble come to a family living in a $100,000 home as well as to one in a run-down shack. As much as we may find wrong with the institutional Church, we still need her desperately!

Nothing on earth or in hell can destroy the Church. Jesus said, "The powers of hell shall not prevail against it" (Matt. 16:18, LB). Throughout the centuries many attempts at destruction have been made. The worst of Satan's attacks have been unleashed against her. But the Church is not going out of style. It is not a relic from the past. Its Founder is still alive and sustains His Church with life and vitality. Denominations rise and fall, but His Church will stand forever! Even the institutional or denominational expression of the Church of Jesus Christ will no doubt endure in some form as long as time lasts.

No one can ever rightly claim ownership of the Church. We must always remember that the Church belongs to Christ. He called it "my church." Regardless of our investments in church properties, the Church does not belong to us. If indeed it is His Church, we must show a proper concern for His will in matters relating to it.

The Body of Christ

What love that Christ should condescend to leave His heavenly throne and indwell human flesh (John 1:14)! For 33 years He shared in every aspect of our humanity. Then evil men took the Best Man who ever lived and snuffed out His life. No longer is He with us in the flesh. Yet He is with us in a different but real way. So real is His presence in the Church that we can say, "The Church is his body" (Eph. 1:23, Phillips).

Thus, the true Church is identified with Christ. Work done for the Church is work done for the Lord. There is no need to feel we must divide our loyalties between Christ and the Church. Loyalty to one is of necessity loyalty to the other. Any contradiction or distinction between winning people to Christ and winning them to the Church is unreal and imaginary. Be careful that you don't let the idea of competition between Christ and the Church arise. The Church is the body of Christ.

The Church as the body of Christ is sometimes described as the universal Church. Its boundaries are not identical with denominational lines. Membership in the universal Church is a divine action: "Every day the Lord added to their number those who were finding salvation" (Acts 2:47, Phillips). Before becoming a member one is expected to make a confession with the lips and heart that Jesus is Lord. Such a confession is necessary for acceptance with God. "Whosoever therefore shall confess me before men, him will I confess also before my Father which is in heaven. But whosoever shall deny me before men, him will I also deny before my Father which is in heaven" (Matt. 10:32-33).

All Christians, regardless of what group they are members of, belong to the body of Christ. Not everyone who belongs to a local church organization is a member of Christ's Church. But, regardless of what local group you belong to, if you know Christ you belong to His Church. Perhaps Christians should more often sing the little chorus:

Oh, I care not what church you belong to,
Just as long as for God you may stand.
We may not have the same rank or title,
But you're my brother, so give me your hand.

As soon as you are saved, you become a member of His Church. If you have confessed Christ as Lord, you already belong to the Church universal. This does not mean that you should not join a local congregation—indeed, you should! But the more important church membership is taken care of when you accept Christ in your heart and life.

Your body is not you, but it is where you live. The Church, as the body of Christ, is not Christ but it embodies Him in a very precious way. Through it He accomplishes His purposes on earth today. As His body, The Church represents Christ. In all our activities as a group called a Church we should strive to see that "He is first in everything" (Col. 1:18, LB). The Church today continues what "Jesus began both to do and teach" (Acts 1:1). The body of Christ must do what Christ would do. What a great responsibility this places on the Church!

No church organization can rightly claim to be the only

"true Church." Anyone claiming a monopoly or a corner on God in this way is demonstrating sheer bigotry. Such a spirit is too little to be becoming to Christ. The great Head of the Church is inclusive in His love and does not seek to exclude anyone. He cannot be restricted to any one group. The boundaries of His Church stretch out to include peoples of all races, ethnic groups, social strata, and church organizations. The invitation of Christ still stands: "Come unto me, *all* ye that labour" (Matt. 11:28, italics mine).

Local churches and denominations have heads of their organizations. Jesus Christ is the Church's Head. In Eph. 1:22-23 we read: "[God] hath put all things under his feet, and gave him to be the head over all things to the church, which is his body, the fulness of him that filleth all in all." Again we read, "He is the head of the body, the church . . . Now I rejoice in my sufferings for your sake, and in my flesh I complete what is lacking in Christ's afflictions for the sake of his body, that is, the church" (Col. 1:18, 24, RSV). Since it is His body, the Church belongs to Him. He possesses the right and power to direct and govern His own body. If Christ is not the Head, it is not a Church but merely a human institution. The head guides and directs the body. In the same way, the Church is under the direction and leadership of Christ.

Christ loves the Church even as a man loves his own body. This truth is made clear in Eph. 5:28. His love is a self-giving, self-sacrificing, sanctifying love. It was this kind of love that took Him to the Cross. Why? "To make her [the Church] holy and clean, washed by baptism and God's Word; so that he could give her to himself a glorious church without a single spot or wrinkle or any other blemish, being holy and without a single fault" (Eph. 5:26-27, LB). That love is just as strong and real today as when Paul penned those words.

The People of God

In the church we have buildings, organizations, councils, assemblies, committees and committees and committees! The danger is that we mistake these necessary outer trappings for the real thing. All of these are helpful to the church, but none of them is the church. At best they are designed only to enable the church to operate effectively. The church at its heart is simply the people of God.

Where is the church located? Of course you answer immediately, "Why, ours is at Main and Cherry Street." You answer that way because almost universally we identify the church building with the church. In most minds they are identical and it seems a trifling, silly thing to say otherwise. It must be seen that this is only the physical building which belongs to the church. How strange that we should confuse the church's real estate with the church itself!

Maybe we would do well to remind ourselves that the earliest Christian Church had no buildings at all. They had no problem with saying the church was at Main and Cherry Street. Yet with no buildings—either ornate or simple—they had a vital, growing Church. The building is the place devoted to Christ's cause for worship and evangelism. Wherever God's people are, that is where the church is located. Yes, on Sunday it may be that the church meets at Main and Cherry, but on Monday morning it is a different story. Then, the church is scattered in a hundred different directions. The church is people—the people of God.

Always, the church is people. All too often we cannot see the trees for the forest. Unfortunately when we look at the church, we sometimes cannot see the people for the buildings . . . and the committees! How easy to forget that the church is people! Writing to the church at Ephesus, Paul addressed them as "the saints at Ephesus" (Eph. 1:1). This is the consistent practice in the New Testament, for everywhere the church is people.

God loves and accepts all kinds of people—and they become the people of God. There has never been a common mold from which they must be shaped. A church may begin without a building, but it cannot begin without people. Until there are people, a church remains a mere dream. In no way does this minimize the need for buildings and organizations. It only places the emphasis where it belongs—on people. The church is people, not a place. It is believers, not a building. People, yes, the people of God.

In the Old Testament, Israel was known as the people of God. To ancient Israel, Moses said, "Thou art an holy people unto the Lord thy God: the Lord thy God hath chosen thee to be a special people unto himself, above all people that are upon the face of the earth. The Lord did not set his love upon you, nor choose you, because ye were more in number than any people; for ye were the fewest of all people: but because the Lord loved you" (Deut. 7:6-8). Israel rejected God, especially God in Jesus Christ. They stumbled over the "rock," and lost their standing as God's special people. In turn, God made a new covenant and elected a new people under the terms of His new covenant. His new Israel has been called the Church. The Israel of God (that is, the people of God) is the Israel defined by God. The Christian Church is vitally related to the people of God in the Old Testament. The Church is but an extension of the people of God.

Peter saw all this and to the new Israel he wrote: "But you are a chosen race, a royal priesthood, a holy nation, God's own people ... Once you were no people but now you are God's people; once you had not received mercy but now you have received mercy" (I Pet. 2:9-10, RSV). What an inspiring thought! God's love and mercy explained the existence of ancient Israel. That same love and mercy is the only adequate explanation for the existence of the Church of Christ today.

I Pet. 2:1-10 is one of the key passages concerning the nature of the Church. Clearly it tells us that the Church of Jesus Christ is now the true Israel of God. Its purpose is the same as that of ancient Israel—to have a community of salvation in the world. Christ crucified was the great stumbling stone for Israel. Because Israel refused to accept Christ, God rejected her as His chosen instrument of bringing salvation to the world. Through the crucificion and resurrection of Jesus Christ, God has created a new Israel—the Church. His chosen people now are those who are "elect" in Jesus Christ.

This passage explains the purpose of the people of God. I Pet. 2:9 echoes Exod. 19:6—"But ye are . . . a royal priesthood." *Pontifex* is the Latin word for "priest" and literally it means "bridge builder." The role of the Church then is to build a bridge so those outside of Christ may come to know Him. Everyone in the Church becomes a priest, helping to bring broken humanity to the foot of the Cross. Bridge building is exciting work when done for God in Christ's name.

This is how Peter put it: "You are God's 'chosen generation,' his 'royal priesthood,' his 'holy nation,' his 'peculiar people'—all the old titles of God's people now belong to you. It is for you now to demonstrate the goodness of him who has called you out of darkness into his amazing light" (I Pet. 2:9, Phillips). The people of God—the Church—exists for the sole purpose of demonstrating the saving power of God. In a sense, we are on display to convince others to trust Him in full commitment.

Christians are termed living stones, "building blocks" (I Pet. 2:5, LB), used to build God's house, the Church. So we are reminded that there is strictly no such thing as "solitary religion." A "free-lance" Christian is a contradiction in terms. Always God's people are a *community* of believers. For this reason every born-again believer should identify with the visible church in his community. A brick by itself remains quite useless. It is when it is used to build a building that its purpose is realized. The individual Christian needs to identify with the community—never stand alone. It is just this community idea which encourages us and reminds us that we are never alone. We are the *people of God!*

Through group effort we can accomplish what none of us can do alone. As the minister says when he receives members into the church, "There is cooperation in service, accomplishing that which cannot otherwise be done" *(Manual,* 1972, p. 310). We need each other and it is through the church that we are united so we can do God's work in a satisfactory manner.

THE FAMILY OF GOD

Closely related to the "people of God" concept is that of the Church as the "family of God." Such symbolism has deep roots in Old Testament thought. Sometimes in the New Testament the word *oikos* means "household" or "family" and not a building (temple or church). This Hebraic thought is carried over in the New Testament in such passages as Heb. 8:8, where we read of "the house of Israel" and "the house of Judah." But Israel is no longer the family of God and thus we read in Heb. 10:21 of "the house of God." In I Pet. 4:17 the same phrase is translated in the *Living Bible* as "God's own children."

Every believer is now considered as one of God's children. "But to all who received him, who believed in his name, he gave power to become children of God" (John 1:12, RSV). If all are children, then collectively we are the "family of God." Through the blood of Christ, not creation, we are all the children of God. The New Testament Church is really the new Israel. His people can no longer be restricted by race or nationality. All of us are a part of the redeemed family of God. You are a child of God through His saving power. You belong to a precious family. "You are members of God's very own family, citizens of God's country" (Eph. 2:19, LB).

Floyd and Joyce Robinson had been saved only a few months. Floyd had given up a lucrative entertainment career to sing the gospel of Jesus Christ. How refreshing at a ministers' breakfast for the Atlanta, Ga., zone to hear the Robinsons speak of the church as "our family." It was Joyce who said, "We're just so glad to meet some more of our brothers and sisters. Everywhere we go we find some more of our family." How right she is!

All of God's children (with the exception of Jesus Christ) are adopted. God has many children but no grandchildren! Adoption is accomplished through Christ's blood and the forgiveness of sins (Eph. 1:5-6). God sent His Son that He might "lead us into becoming, by adoption, true sons of God" (Gal. 4:5, Phillips). Again Paul reminds us, "Ye have received the Spirit of adoption, whereby we cry, Abba, Father" (Rom. 8:15). Phillips paraphrases that verse so beautifully: "You have been adopted into the very family circle of God and you can say with a full heart, 'Father, my Father.'" We must always remember that we are children by adoption. It is through mercy and grace and love that it is so. Nothing we have done merited us this favored position; it is all of God and all of love.

There is "one God and Father of all" (Eph. 2:6). We are all brothers and sisters in God's family. Whenever you meet another Christian, you are meeting a brother or sister. God has only one family. It was Christ who broke down "the dividing wall of hostility" (Eph. 2:14, RSV). Jews and Gentiles need no longer to be enemies. At the Cross, Jesus "fused" them together as "one new person" (Eph. 2:15, LB). Regardless of race, nationality, or church affiliation, God's children are brothers and sisters.

In the family you find support, love, and strength.

There is mutual respect and trust. You are free to confess your faults, failures, and shortcomings without censure. In such an atmosphere you are able to open your life to the healing forces of God. From your brothers and sisters in Christ you receive encouragement and the sense of belonging. The collective strength of God's family is yours.

Love is the one essential characteristic of the family, especially God's family. The royal law is love (Jas. 2:8). This is the "old commandment" that was retained by the Christian family (I John 2:7-8). The most important thing to be said to any church is simply, "Love one another." The Church knows the kind of love John was talking about. He put it bluntly: "Let us stop just *saying* we love people; let us *really* love them, and *show* it by our *actions*" (I John 3:18, LB). Nothing finer can be said of the Church than, "Behold how they love one another!" The popular song has it put in this fashion, "What the world needs now is love, sweet love." In the Church that love may be found. It is the love of brothers and sisters—the family of God.

The Early Church pointed the way for us to act as a family. Read about it in Acts 4:32-37. What one had, they all had. "And no one felt that what he owned was his own" (Acts 4:32, LB). Everyone shared and shared alike. No doubt this would present problems if we tried to duplicate this behavior in the Church today. But at least it does demononstrate in a positive way that the Church at its best is a family.

Jesus considered all Christians to be members of His family. Once while He was teaching in Capernaum, His mother and brothers came and sought audience with Him. Using this occasion as an opportunity for teaching, Jesus asked the informers to define who is "my mother" and "my brethren" (Mark 3:33). Then He gave His own definition by looking around at the crowd and saying, "These are my mother and brothers! Anyone who does God's will is my brother, and my sister, and my mother" (Mark 3:34-35, LB). Significantly, He did not include "Father" in that list. Christ has only one Father, but many brothers and sisters. Following His example, we too know that all Christians everywhere are our brothers and sisters. How thrilling, comforting, and strengthening to be a member of this unique family of God!

LIKE A MIGHTY ARMY

Some churches have quit singing it. Others have deleted it from their hymnals. There is the claim that it sounds too much like war for the Church of Jesus Christ. Regardless of these superficial claims, the song the Church should sing with real meaning is, "Like a mighty army moves the Church of God." That militancy and determination have always characterized the true Church of Jesus Christ.

Some wag has parodied this militant song of the Church so that it reads:

Like a mighty tortoise moves the Church of God;
Brothers, we are treading where we've always trod.

In too many quarters of the Church the parody fits better than the original! But biblical language describes the Church as an army. Paul tells the Church, "You must therefore be [like men] stripped for action" (I Pet. 1:13, NEB).

The Quaker philosopher Elton Trueblood affirms that the Church "must be a fellowship of the committed."[1] Such language tends to fall on deaf ears today. We prefer not to hear Jesus calling His followers to daily take up a cross (Luke 9:23). Ease and comfort have made Christians soft. But the Church of Jesus Christ needs and must resemble a military band. Commitment and militancy should ever be the trademarks of God's people.

In another of his books, Trueblood begins by saying, "Committed Christians are a minority at the present time."[2] Compiling all our "success" stories will never erase that fact.

Building great cathedrals and enormous increases in membership and income do not make the Church what it should be. It is shameful that illustrations of commitment today come from the Communistic, radical sectors or from some religious cult. Can it be that fear of fanaticism has diluted us so that we are less the Church than we should be?

The greatest single alternative to Christianity, Trueblood says, is "a conventionalized association with the Christian heritage which is best described as mild religion."[3] Mild religion was never God's intention for His Church. Interestingly enough, in church history it can be noted that God has continually raised up new groups with a militant attitude and real religious fervor. When a church begins to lose its zeal and "fire," you may be sure God will raise another to take its place.

Paul admonishes the Christian to "endure hardness, as a good soldier of Jesus Christ" (II Tim. 2:3). From his letter to the Ephesians, one gets the idea that Paul thought of the Church as an army. "Put on all of God's armor so that you will be able to stand safe against all strategies and tricks of Satan. For we are not fighting against people made of flesh and blood, but against persons without bodies—the evil rulers of the unseen world, those mighty satanic beings and great evil princes of darkness who rule this world; and against huge numbers of wicked spirits in the spirit world. So use every piece of God's armor to resist the enemy whenever he attacks, and when it is all over, you will still be standing up. But to do this, you will need the strong belt of truth and the breastplate of God's approval. Wear shoes that are able to speed you on as you preach the Good News of peace with God. In every battle you will need faith as your shield to stop the fiery arrows aimed at you by Satan. And you will need the helmet of salvation and the sword of the Spirit—which is the Word of God" (Eph. 6:11-17, LB).

The Church is more than a "useful" institution in the

community. It is more than just a place to dedicate babies, baptize church members, perform weddings, and conduct funerals. The Church is more than a "service center" when folk need certain "services." Of its membership, total commitment and involvement are required. The commitment is to Jesus Christ, the Church's Founder, and the involvement is in service for God. This will always include doing the work of evangelism. Almost fanatical devotion and zeal for its cause are required. So Jesus said the way was "narrow" and only a "few" would enter. But what wonderful fellowship in "the company of the commited"!

When the Church acts like an army, everyone is an evangelist. In the Early Church everyone was an evangelist. The New Testament Church has no spectators sitting on the sidelines! All are soldiers engaged in mortal conflict. God's grace is not for ornamentation; it is for service.

Evangelism is the purpose of the Church's existence. No other cause justifies its continuance. Unless the Church engages in the battle for souls, it will die. It will cease to be the Church and God will be obliged to create a new "people of God." The late Dr. Samuel Shoemaker, an Episcopal minister, reminded us that "there is no Church where evangelism is not living and current."[4] Such an evangelistic band will surely resemble in some respects an army. Wherever the Church of Jesus Christ is found, it will be behaving like an army arrayed for battle.

Everything in this life has a price tag on it. Membership in Christ's Church is no exception. What cost God such an infinite price cannot come cheap for us. And, really, the kingdom of God—the pearl of great price or the Church of Jesus Christ—is cheap at any cost. No price is too high for a vital, living relationship with God. That is precisely the prerequisite for membership in His Church. Reginald Heber reminds us of that cost and challenges us with the words of his hymn:

A glorious band, the chosen few
  On whom the Spirit came!
Twelve valiant saints, their hope they knew
  And mocked the cross and flame;
They met the tyrant's brandished steel,
  The lion's gory mane;
They bowed their necks the death to feel.
  Who follows in their train?

ONE TRUE CHURCH

There is one true Church of Jesus Christ. No one denomination is that church. All of God's people everywhere are rightfully members of the one true Church. Since Calvary there is "one body, and one Spirit . . . one Lord, one faith, one baptism, one God and Father of all" (Eph. 4:4-6).

In His high-priestly prayer, Jesus prayed for the unity of the Church. He prayed that "they all may be one" (John 17:21). As His followers, in obedience to His command, assembled in the Upper Room they were "with one accord" (Acts 2:1). It was in such a spirit of unity that the Church was born. H. Orton Wiley reminds us, "Pentecost was the birthday of the Church."[5] It is the Spirit and power of Pentecost that keeps the Church united. So long as the Holy Spirit has control there will be unity. "So we, being many, are one body in Christ, and every one members one of another" (Rom. 12:5).

This is Paul's putting of the matter: "Just as there are many parts to our bodies, so it is with Christ's body. We are all parts of it, and it takes every one of us to make it complete, for we each have different work to do. So we belong to each other, and each needs all the others" (Rom. 12:4-5, LB).

A well-functioning body must have unity. All the parts (groups and individuals) must work together. Each has a role to play and a job to do. We must realize that we are parts one of another and that we all belong to the same body. Our goal is the same and all of us serve the same living Lord. We need one another and should take advantage of every opportunity for cooperative efforts in God's work. The Church of God is not a little, cliquish, isolationist clan. It is a big outfit, including men of every race and clime.

The local church is but the Church universal in miniature, to the extent that it remains true to the nature of Christ's body. So there must be spiritual unity in the local church. Everyone is needed; no one needs to feel unwanted or unnecessary. One member is just as important as another. All the parts of the body are needed.

Now the floodlight focuses in on you! Paul would remind you: "Don't cherish exaggerated ideas of yourself or your importance" (Rom. 12:3, Phillips). But in the next breath, he exhorts you to "try to have a sane estimate of your capabilities" (Rom. 12:3, Phillips). You are important in the Church and you are needed. Have a sane estimate of your abilities and gifts. Use whatever God has given you for His glory and the good of the Church. Don't hide behind a false humility.

Accept yourself as a child of God and as a part of the ongoing Church of Jesus Christ. You are not inferior; neither are you superior. No one person is able to do all that is necessary to the life of the Church. To the degree that you lag behind, the Church will lag. By the same token, the Church will progress to the same degree that you do your best with what God has given you. Is the general the only good soldier on the battlefield? To be sure, he is not! Every recruit at the battle front has a job, and the total job will not be done unless every man does his part.

A fallacy easy to fall into is that of assuming that one job in the church is more important than another. Paul gives a humorous twist to this. "Yes, the body has many parts, not just one part. If the foot says, 'I am not a part of the body because I am not a hand,' that does not make it any less a part of the body. And what would you think if you heard an ear say, 'I am not part of the body because I am only an ear, and not an eye'? Would that make it any less a part of the body? Suppose the whole body were an eye—then how would you hear? Or if your whole body were just one big ear, how could you smell anything? . . . The eye can never say to the hand, 'I don't need you.' The head can't say to the feet, 'I don't need you.' And some of the parts that seem weakest and least important are really the most necessary" (I Cor. 12:14-17, 21-22, LB). Each has a different role to play and each is vitally necessary to the whole. You are important in the church to which you belong.

Members of the Church are so bound up in their lives together that they are inseparable. "If one part suffers, all parts suffer with it, and if one part is honored, all the parts are glad" (I Cor. 12:26, LB). When one member hurts anywhere (mentally, emotionally, physically, or spiritually), all the others hurt with him. If one member has cause for joy and rejoicing, everyone in the body has cause for rejoicing. We hurt together; we cry together. We rejoice and laugh together. Sharing one another's burdens and sunshine is the nature of the Church. It is inconceivable that the Church would ever do otherwise.

How wonderful and marvelous is the Church! She is God's own creation; she is the body of Jesus Christ. Within the Church millions of souls have found shelter and refuge. The Church has provided strength and solace through the ages to all who have availed themselves of her strength. Trying to take it all in, one finds Timothy Dwight's hymn coming to mind:

> *I love Thy kingdom, Lord,*
> *The house of Thine abode,*
> *The Church our blest Redeemer saved*
> *With His own precious blood.*

For Your Consideration

1. How would you distinguish between denominations and the Church of Jesus Christ?

2. What is the rock upon which Jesus builds His Church?

3. Discuss the concept of the Church as the body of Christ.

4. Read in several of the modern English translations I Pet. 2:1-10. Explain in your own words the concept of the church as "the people of God."

5. How do we become a part of the "family of God"?

6. When is the Church most "like a mighty army"?

Chapter 3

Meet the Nazarenes

"Who are these Nazarenes?" They are all kinds of people. No two are exactly alike. They are the kind of people living in your neighborhood.

Some are short . . . some are tall.
Some are older . . . some are younger.
Some are married . . . some are single.
Some drive Cadillacs . . . some drive Volkswagens.
Some are wealthy . . . some are poor.
Some are white . . . some are black or yellow.
Some are laborers . . . some hold managerial positions.

There are doctors, nurses, lawyers, farmers, and many others in their ranks. College professors and those with little or no education add to the diversity of their complexion. They play golf, tennis, and baseball. You can find them everywhere. Around the world you find them—more than 500,000 of them! People, yes, they are all kinds of people.

Yet, wherever they are, there are some distinctives which mark them. When you begin talking about their religious life, these differences surface. It is never easy to characterize a group. The diversity of cultures, races, ethnic and social backgrounds of the great host of Nazarenes around the world adds to this difficulty. Still some characterization must be attempted if you are to know who the Nazarenes are.

THEY ARE CHRISTIANS

No off-brand cult are they. Nazarenes are clearly in the mainstream of historic Christianity. The Church of the Nazarene proudly takes her place alongside other Christian denominations. None of her leaders ever claimed she was the only true Church. Nazarenes realize that the Church of Jesus Christ is the only true Church. This is the Church that includes every Christian on earth and every saint in heaven. Within that body of Christ, Nazarenes gladly find themselves.

As a denomination, the Church of the Nazarene readily acknowledges the primacy of the Church of Jesus Christ. When her ministers are ordained, they are "set apart and ordained an Elder in the Church of God, according to the rules of the Church of the Nazarene" (*Manual*, par. 698.1). Although there are definite distinctives, Nazarenes choose to be identified as Christians and thus with the universal Church of Jesus Christ.

The Church of the Nazarene is a Protestant denomination. Historically Nazarenes are inheritors of the Protestant tradition. Neither a cult nor a sect, the church is thoroughly a Protestant organization. Her historical roots reach back through the Methodist church to John Wesley and right on back to the apostles. Perhaps in her younger years she might have been considered a sect, but this no longer is true.

Theologically the Church of the Nazarene is conservative. Nazarenes, however, disclaim any association with "Fundamentalism." The defensive attitude and pietistic isolationist tendency of Fundamentalists cause Nazarenes to wish not to be known by that name. While conservative, the church is neither fanatical nor contentious. Probably it would be best described as a middle-of-the-road conservative church. Its conservative stance has usually been applied also to its ethics and standards.

Doctrinally the church is Wesleyan. Entire sanctification is the distinctive tenet of its creed. Sanctification is taught and preached as a second definite work of divine grace. The doctrine is not taught, however, simply because Wesley taught it. It is a biblical doctrine which has historically come to be thought of as a Wesleyan doctrine. This is because John Wesley rediscovered this great biblical truth.

They Are "Holiness People"

This fact is clearly indicated by Timothy L. Smith, official church historian, in *Called unto Holiness.* He begins the Nazarene story with the holiness revival of 1858-88. Dr. P. F. Bresee, the church's founder, often said the Church of the Nazarene was born in the holiness revival. From the very beginning "the chief aim of the church was to preach holiness to the poor."[1]

Following the Civil War the holiness revival swept the entire country. There were those who refused to have the fire of the Holy Spirit snuffed out in ritual and liturgy. Often ministers and laymen found themselves "frozen out" of old-line denominations. Sometimes they were forthrightly asked to quit their professions of holiness or get out.

Contrary to common belief, the Church of the Nazarene is not a schism or "split off" from the Methodist church. The holiness base was extremely broad both denominationally and geographically. Holiness bands which merged into the Church of the Nazarene were to be found in the East, South, West, and North. The one thing they all had in common was the desire to spread scriptural holiness. This overwhelming desire forged them together, allowing them to forego many of their petty differences.

Many denominational backgrounds get into the picture: P. F. Bresee, Methodist; William Howard Hoople, Baptist; Edward F. Walker, Presbyterian; J. O. McClurkan, Cumberland Presbyterian; A. M. Hills and George Sharpe, of Scotland, Congregationalists; Edgar P. Ellyson and Seth C. Rees were Friends; and John W. Goodwin was an Advent Christian. From even such sketchy information, one may readily see that there was no "split off" from any denomination. There was a coming together of strong holiness leaders from all parts of the country and from many of the major denominations of America.

At times during the crisis years of the formation of the church, there was the serious question of "come-outism." Some of the outstanding holiness leaders felt that the sanctified should remain in the older denominations and be loyal witnesses there. Others, equally as sanctified, felt they could not afford to stay where they were not wanted and their experience was not appreciated. Many of these formed interdenominational holiness bands even while remaining within their churches. From these bands of holiness people the Church of the Nazarene was born.

"Holiness" means many things to different people. Because of this, many well-intentioned people are afraid to even talk about holiness. For Nazarenes, holiness is in no way associated with wildfire fanaticism. They do not believe speaking in tongues is an evidence of the baptism of the Holy Spirit. Handling of snakes and fire play no part in the doctrine for Nazarenes. Neither is it to be equated with legalistic religion nor offbeat, bizarre behavior. Weird misconceptions of holiness have scared many people. Holiness should in no way be thought of as super pietism.

God "is holy," Peter declares (I Pet. 1:15). Really this is nothing new, for this same note is sounded in Lev. 11:44-46; 19:2; 20:7, 26. Thus a holy God demands that His people be holy like himself (I Pet. 1:15). This is not optional or elective equipment. It is not excess baggage. Holiness is God's requirement for every Christian. God calls all men to holiness (I Thess. 4:7). Therefore, without apology, Nazarenes call themselves "holiness people." Unofficially, "Called unto Holiness" has become the theme song of the church. In nearly every district and general church meeting you will hear the people sing this tremendous hymn.

Basically, holiness is purity of heart and life (cf. Matt. 5:8). It means to be cleansed from all sin (I John 1:7). Holiness as an experience bring back God's perfect love to the soul (Rom. 5:5; I John 4:17-18). Far from being an offbeat tune, this restores a man to his God-intended state. Biblical holiness is practical; it is for man wherever he is. God's command is to "be holy in every department of your lives" (I Pet. 1:15, Phillips).

Various terms are used interchangeably for holiness. Some of these include, "sanctification," "perfect love," "the baptism with the Holy Spirit," "the fullness of the Spirit," "entire sanctification," and others. Probably "perfect love" describes holiness as well as any other term. Biblical holiness is I Corinthians 13 at work in one's life daily. It becomes positive love, such as the Good Samaritan exemplified.

Nazarenes do not believe that holiness renders the sanctified unable to sin again. They do not believe that holiness places believers above or beyond the ability to make mistakes. Even the entirely sanctified will still be tempted, for he remains human even though he is holy. Even though holiness people sometimes use the term "Christian perfection" for holiness, they do not mean by this that there is no room left for improvement in the sanctified life. Certainly they do not intend ever to have a "holier than thou" attitude in regard to non-holiness people.

They do believe the Holy Spirit can cleanse the heart of the believer from all evil tendencies to sin. If one is filled with the Holy Spirit, there is no reason or necessity for sinning. The Spirit-filled Christian does not sin every day in word, thought, and deed. Sinning is not an inherent part of humanity, as some would have us believe. Daily sinning and nightly repenting should have no place in the life of the sanctified. Perfected in love—in motive and intention (cf. Matt. 5:48)—the wholly sanctified wants nothing but the whole will of God for his life. Should a sanctified person sin, as is possible, he may immediately repent and never break his close fellowship with Jesus Christ (I John 2:1).

Reduced to its simplest definition, holiness is Christlikeness. Unless we have the Spirit of Christ, we are none of His (Rom. 8:9). We are "hid with Christ in God" (Col. 1:3). Holiness is the spirit and life of Christ incarnated in human flesh. It is Christlikeness begun and growing daily. As Wesley said, it is "the life of God in the soul; the image of God fresh stamped on the heart; an entire renewal of the mind in every temper and thought after the likeness of Him that created it." Nazarenes believe that Jesus came to introduce an age when God's people might "serve him without fear, in holiness and righteousness" (Luke 1:74-75).

The leaders of the church never intended that holiness would become a religion of legalistic rules. There are freedom and joy in the life of holiness. Holiness should release one from bondage, not place him under the servitude of a legalistic system! The Holy Spirit is eminently more qualified to dictate matters of conscience than is an ecclesiastical body. Spirit-filled Christians should not need the legislation of standards. According to Dr. Timothy L. Smith, the church was early characterized by the fact that "its discipline depended primarily upon the work of the Holy Spirit."[2] The Church of the Nazarene remains to this day a holiness church.

THEY ARE EVANGELISTIC

Born and nurtured in the fires of revival, the Church of the Nazarene remains an intensely evangelistic church. Dr.

Bresee wanted centers of holy fire in every great city in the nation. Such revival centers did develop and because of them the church has grown at an amazing rate. To be true to their name, holiness people must be characterized by witnessing (cf. Acts 1:8). Without a strong witness for Christ, claims to holiness are nullified. Throughout the Book of Acts the infilling of the Spirit brings a spirit of evangelism.

Revivalism is still considered by Nazarenes as a valid means of evangelism. Most of her churches will have at least two revival campaigns each year. Sometimes these are called evangelistic crusades as a way of updating the terminology. But mass evangelism is not limited to such special occasions. The Sunday evening service is usually called the "Sunday evening evangelistic service." Often the evangelistic fervor will be evident in the morning services as well.

The altar is a prominent piece of furniture in Nazarene churches. Its purpose is the same as the old-fashioned "mourners' bench." As a rule, Churches of the Nazarene will not settle for a Communion rail to replace the altar. Most services are closed with an invitation for those with spiritual needs to come and pray. Confession of sin is made to God, not to the minister or altar workers. Repentance is urged upon those wanting to receive Christ as Saviour. There is often weeping as one under deep conviction seeks the forgiveness that only God can bring. Seekers are urged then to publicly confess Christ.

Persons saved at the altar in the Church of the Nazarene are not automatically members of the church. The call for repentance is not an invitation to join the church. Nazarenes believe that one's relationship to God is of prime importance. When one is sure that his sins are forgiven and he has met the requirements for membership, he is urged to unite with the church. The importance of church membership is not played down. It is only placed in its proper focus by delaying church membership until one has received Christ into his heart.

Sermons, especially in the evening services, will be of the evangelistic type—that is, the kind of preaching designed to bring a decision for Christ. This does not mean the preacher must "rant and rave." Although he was an evangelist at heart, Dr. Bresee was one of the first men of his generation to consistently use the conversational style of preaching. He looked at his audience and preached as though he were talking with one person alone.

In our evangelism, salvation is declared as a personal responsibility and privilege. It is personal encounter with, and submission to, Christ as Lord. Reaching for the heart as well as the mind, the minister may become emotional in his plea for repentance unto life. This does not mean that he will take advantage of a congregation.

Evangelism is not confined to the walls of the church. Nazarenes are urged to become personal soul winners. Evangelism is everyone's business. Everyone who joins the Church of the Nazarene promises to become a soul winner. That vow is found in the General Rules of the *Manual*. It reads like this: "Pressing upon the attention of the unsaved the claims of the gospel, inviting them to the house of the Lord, and trying to compass their salvation" (p. 39).

Quite often classes on personal evangelism will be taught in Nazarene churches. Instruction in the art and techniques of leading someone to Christ is given. Classes of this sort sometimes include "practice sessions" to help younger Christians learn how to lead another person to Christ. Sermons on witnessing are not uncommon. Their purpose most often is to bring a commitment on the part of Christians to win others for Christ.

Evangelism is primary and foremost for Nazarenes. Its base is broader in this church than in many others. Not only do they press upon unbelievers the claims of the gospel, but they urge the ones who have been saved to seek sanctification. "Holiness evangelism" has an important place in the church. This is so important that revivals are sometimes called "holiness meetings" or, more commonly now, "holiness conventions."

They Are a Singing People

From its inception the Church of the Nazarene has been a singing church. Every growing Nazarene church is known as a church in love with music. There is no hesitancy in using songs with the pronoun "I." Testimony-type songs are prominent in the services. Experience-centered hymns tell what God has done for the believer.

Cantatas and anthems are also used, but to a more limited extent. Gospel music with a message for the heart is far more characteristic in Nazarene services. Nazarene music is at its best in an evangelistic atmosphere. The singing is usually lighter and faster in tempo than in non-evangelistic churches. Such music is clearly justifiable in a church which by its own admission is an evangelistic church. People are urged to sing "in the Spirit." This kind of singing prepares the way for the evangelistic message and the invitation to seek Christ.

A strong emphasis is placed on congregational singing. This could not be otherwise since we stress the priesthood of all believers in our theology. Everyone is encouraged to "get in on the act" of worship. Nothing stirs the heart to worship so well as good, hearty congregational singing. Worshippers are encouraged to participate, not merely to sit in as spectators. When the great hymns of the Church are sung with simplicity and fervor, they create a profound spirit of reverence in the heart of the worshipper. Through the medium of the gospel song all the people are given a voice with which to express their religious emotions.

Music has been used for evangelistic purposes since the

days of Martin Luther. With his new music and congregational singing he won many to the Reformation faith. Sometimes whole cities were won in a day with his music. "It is extremely significant that Martin Luther, who led the Reformation, was also the first evangelical hymn writer."[3] Nazarene music is clearly in the Reformation tradition.

Doctrine is learned by the common man as he sings. Theologians argue fine points of doctrine, but the common man sings his affirmations of faith. There is value in the continued repetition of our cardinal doctrines through the medium of music. "The friends as well as the enemies of the Reformation asserted that the spread of the new doctrines was due more to Luther's hymns than his sermons."[4] One pope has been quoted as saying, "That monk [Luther] conquers us not by his speech, but by his songs."

Nazarenes insist on singing the songs of their faith. Personal salvation, holiness, and the glory of walking with Jesus are the themes they employ. More holiness theology can be taught through the singing of hymns than through the preaching of the doctrine. Dr. Leslie Parrott quotes a general superintendent as saying, "We must sing our way into the hearts of sin-sick humanity."[5] Thus our singing has a two-fold purpose: to win the lost and to teach the saved the doctrines of our faith.

They Are a Worshipping People

While many churches have long had only one service a week, Nazarenes continue to have at least three services every week. There is a worship service on Sunday morning, the evening evangelistic service, and the midweek prayer service. Members and friends are urged to attend all of these services regularly. Every service has a definite purpose and none is considered as optional.

Worship for Nazarenes does not mean stilted, starchy ritualism. There is usually an order of service, but Nazarenes can hardly be described as ritualistic or liturgical. Nazarene worship is somewhere between the informal and ritualistic, avoiding both extremes. Freedom of the Spirit is always desired. No effort is made to repress the emotional element of worship. Demonstrations in the Spirit are never out of place.

Nazarenes feel free to express their religious emotions during a service. If one feels like weeping, crying, laughing, or shouting, he is free to do so. This does not mean the services are disorderly. It does mean that the Spirit has complete control. No order of service has preeminence over the leadership of the Holy Spirit.

"Keeping the glory down" has been the aim of Nazarenes since Bresee's day. That has never been interpreted by the Nazarenes to mean cheap, shallow emotionalism. Just the same, "Amens," "Hallelujahs," and "Praise the Lord's" are often heard in Nazarene worship services. "The glory" is the presence of the Lord and comes with a revelation of the good news in Jesus Christ. Dr. Bresee was famous for his display of holy enthusiasm. He used simple choruses and popular hymns to create a sense of emotional expectancy in all the services. Following his example, the congregation would often clap their hands while singing.

Worship in the Nazarene church features heartfelt singing. Usually there will be one or more special numbers. Prayers will normally be spontaneous and extemporaneous. Any service, without warning or planning, may have a sprinkling of testimonies of God's saving grace. If the Spirit so leads, any service may change its direction. Worship for these people is a joyful, delightful experience. They believe they should leave church feeling a bit different than when they came.

Preaching is central in Nazarene worship. Even the architecture of the church will tell you this. The podium or pulpit for the minister is placed centrally at the front of the sanctuary. Nazarenes believe the Bible is the Word of God. They take seriously what it has to say to them. Ministers in her church must profess to be "called" of God to preach. Thus with a divine message and a divinely called messenger, the proclaimed Word becomes vitally important. Bible-centered preaching has characterized the Nazarene ministry from the beginning. Preaching is usually simple and direct with attention being given to the specific needs of the congregation. The message is usually closed by a song of invitation for those with spiritual needs to come forward and pray.

There is little ritualism in the Church of the Nazarene. Worship is more spontaneous and from the heart. For example, prayers are not "repeated" or "said"; they are prayed. Not even the "Doxology" or the "Apostles' Creed" is used in every service. This does not mean that the church has no ritual. Indeed, the wedding ceremony, baptismal service, Communion service, and reception of new members follow set rituals. Depending on the local pastor, even these rituals may be varied considerably.

Holy Communion or the Lord's Supper is certainly a part of Nazarene worship. Nazarenes, however, feel no compulsion to receive Communion every Lord's Day. Ministers are *required* to serve their congregations Communion *at least* quarterly. Again, depending on the pastor and the local situation, this may be done more often. Certainly Nazarenes believe Communion is important and not to be taken lightly.

THEY ARE GENEROUS GIVERS

Nazarenes are generous with God and their church financially. Sometimes they outgive themselves. For several years they have led all Protestant denominations of 100,000 or more in per capita giving. For the year 1973 the per capita giving for the denomination was $273.75.

Tithing is not compulsory for church membership. It is, however, taught and preached as a biblical principle of giving. And as a rule, when a new person joins the church he is given a box of tithing envelopes. A high percentage of the people in the average Nazarene church regularly tithe their income. In addition, they are liberal in giving for other offerings. To indicate how much Nazarenes believe in tithing, local churches are asked to tithe their total income for the General Budget. About 80 percent of this goes directly to world evangelism.

Twice each year Nazarenes are asked to give sacrificially for world evangelism. A special offering is taken each Easter and Thanksgiving. These offerings get larger every year, while many denominations report declining income for missions. Many churches go well beyond the 10 percent for missions. This kind of generous financial support from Nazarenes amounts to well over $6 million a year.

The heart of stewardship is total commitment. Perhaps their theology of heart holiness contributes to the generous spirit of the Nazarenes. They know everything really belongs to God; thus tithing is no real issue. They can be counted on to support revivals, give for special projects, and for special needs that arise.

Within the context of holiness you find the most meaningful approach to stewardship. Total commitment is the first step in both holiness and stewardship. The sanctified person can live with an eye single to the glory of God. Self-life ceases and Christ becomes the supreme Motivator in his life. With a solid commitment to holiness, Nazarenes cannot afford to be stingy with God and their church. That would be inconsistent with their faith.

Should You Join the Church?

You can now say you know pretty much what Nazarenes are like. Later you will become acquainted with their history and you will take a closer look at their beliefs. But surely already you are asking, Should I join the church? This is certainly a question facing every new convert. He must do something with that question.

Nazarenes do believe in church membership. They place priority on one's relationship with Christ. Before inviting you to join the church they will want to know that you have accepted Christ into your heart and life. But they do believe that you should join a church. They invite you to join their church with the hope that it will bless you as it has them.

Yes, you should join the church! You would not want to live in a community where there was no church, would you? Well, if everyone takes the attitude that he will not join, there will be no church. We join everything else, don't we? Then why neglect the one area of supreme worth? You need the church and the church needs you. Christians must join the church if they want her to continue in existence.

What is more, you should join a holiness church! That is, you should if you want holiness to continue to be preached. If you would like the message of full salvation—holiness—to die, then don't join a holiness church.

You should join the church because you need the strength that comes from the family of believers. You need the support of your brothers and sisters in Christ. To belong to such a "company of the committed" will prove a source of strength and solace to you. The fellowship of Christian comrades gives an added dimension to your life. Each new member is reminded when he joins the Church of the Nazarene that "there is in it such hallowed fellowship as cannot otherwise be known" *(Manual)*.

There is cooperation in service through the church that would involve you in God's work. All that needs to be done cannot be done by single individuals. Teamwork and cooperative effort are required. New Nazarenes are advised that "there is cooperation in service, accomplishing that which cannot otherwise be done." Get hooked up with something bigger than yourself. Join the Church of the Nazarene!

By now you may be asking the age-old question: Can I be a Christian without joining the church? The answer is a qualified yes, with some definite reservations. It's something like being:

> A student who will not go to school.
> A soldier who will not join an army.
> A citizen who will not pay taxes or vote.
> A salesman with no customers.
> An explorer with no base camp.
> A seaman on a ship without a crew.
> A businessman on a deserted island.
> An author without readers.
> A tuba player without a supporting band.
> A parent without a family.
> A football player without a team.
> A politician who is a hermit.
> A scientist who does not share his findings.
> A bee without a hive.[6]

Now really, what kind of Christian would that be? Who wants to try being a Christian without joining the church? That's like trying to be an insurance policy holder without paying the premiums! Get in, get involved, and enjoy the rich blessings of God through your church.

A Democratic People

Government in the Church of the Nazarene is best described as representative. Thus the extremes of both episcopacy and congregational rule are avoided. It is the people who rule in this church. At every level of church government, the people are represented and have a voice. The opinions of the laymen are considered valuable. Laymen actually have a much greater voice in the affairs of the church than does the ordained ministry.

The Local Church. Each local church is governed by an official church board. Members of this board are elected by the congregation at its annual church meeting. The church board is composed of a board of trustees and a board of stewards. *Manual* requirements say there must be at least three of each on the board. The pastor is chairman of the board by virtue of his office. He does not vote on matters brought before the board except in the case of a tie.

Each of the auxiliaries of the church has its own governing body. Members of the congregation at their annual meeting elect a church school board. Primarily its duties relate to the operation of the church school (or Sunday school) in the local church. In many cases now the church school board is the educational committee, which serves as an integral part of the church board. The NYPS (Nazarene Young People's Society) and NWMS (Nazarene World Missionary Society) have their own councils to govern their activities.

Some matters are considered of such importance that the church board cannot make the decision. It must make recommendations and let the church, at a called church meeting, make the choice. Purchasing property is one of the areas where the congregational vote is required. Relocation of a church must be approved by vote of the entire congregation at a called church meeting.

Calling a pastor is another matter that comes before the congregation. With the approval and advice of the district superintendent, the church board nominates a minister to be pastor of the church. A two-thirds majority vote of all members present (15 years of age and older) at a called or annual meeting is required to elect a pastor. He is called for one year the first time. A renewal call can be extended by a two-thirds majority of the members present and of voting age. If there is not a two-thirds majority, but a simple majority vote is given, the pastor may remain but cannot be voted on again without another nomination from the church board.

A congregation may now give a pastor an extended call of two, three, or four years. This, however, is possible only at the time of a renewal vote for the pastor. He must first be elected for one year by a two-thirds majority of the voting members present before the extended call can be presented. The congregation, not the district superintendent or the general superintendent, decides who a church's pastor will be.

Each year, within 60 days prior to the disctrict assembly, the local church has its annual meeting. Officers of the church board and the pastor must give written reports to the congregation on their activities for the year. New officers for the coming church year are elected. Business not otherwise taken care of is considered at the annual meeting. A member of the church must have reached his fifteenth birthday before he can vote. The pastor presides as the chairman of the annual meeting.

The District Church. Each geographical district is governed by the district assembly. The boundaries for the district are determined by the General Assembly. A district assembly has a purpose comparable to the annual church meeting for the local church. Delegates are elected to the district assembly at the annual church meeting by the local congregation. The district assembly meets once a year. The district superintendent and all other district officers are elected at this time. A general superintendent having jurisdiction over the district presides at the district assembly.

Parallel to the local church board, there is a district advisory board. Its membership is 50 percent lay and 50 percent ministerial. During the year, the business of the district is conducted by the district superintendent and the district advisory board. Like the local church, the district has a church school board as well as an NYPS council and an NWMS council. There are at present (1972) 78 districts in the United States, Canada, and the British Isles.

The election of a district superintendent is done at the district assembly. He is elected in a similar manner as the pastor. The main difference is that he is nominated by a nominating ballot. Such election is conducted by the presiding general superintendent. It is to the district superintendent that pastors and congregations look for leadership. When there is a vacancy in a pastorate, he helps the church board and congregation in calling a new pastor. General oversight of the work of the entire district is his responsibility.

Ordination of ministers is an interesting and glorious climax of each district assembly. To be considered, a candidate must be recommended by the local church of which he is a member or by the district advisory board. This nomination must be approved by the board of orders and relations. He must also have completed his course of study and have served in the ministry for at least two years. The presiding general superintendent ordains him as all the elders of the district lay hands on his head. Thus he is set apart a minister "in the Church of God according to the rules of the Church of the Nazarene."

The General Church. True to pattern, at this level too the people still rule. That is, the elected representatives from each district (known as delegates) compose the governing body of the general church. They are made up of half ministers and half laymen. This body is known as the General Assembly. It is analogous to the district assembly and the annual meeting. The General Assembly convenes every four years. The General Assembly elects as many general superintendents as it deems necessary. It also elects a general secretary, general treasurer, and editor of the *Herald of Holiness*. They also elect the members of various boards, such as the trustees of the Nazarene Theological Seminary and Nazarene Bible College. The General Board, which governs the church between General Assemblies, is elected by the General Assembly.

A general superintendent holds the highest elective office in the church. He is elected by a two-thirds majority vote of the General Assembly. The general superintendents, of which there are six, working together as a board, have general supervision of the Church of the Nazarene. They preside jointly and severally over the General Assembly and the meetings of the General Board. They ordain ministers as elders. A general superintendent presides over each district assembly. When a vacancy occurs in the district superintendency, the general superintendents, after consultation with the advisory board, may appoint a new one.

Similar to the local church board and the district advisory board, the general church has a General Board. As stated, the members of the General Board are elected by the General Assembly. When the General Assembly is not in session, this board takes care of the business of the general church under the supervision of the general superintendents. It elects the executive secretaries of the eight departments and directors of general commissions, the manager of the Nazarene Publishing House, and the stewardship secretary. One of its most interesting duties is the appointment of missionaries. The missionary candidate is nominated by the Department of World Missions with the approval of the Board of General superintendents.

The General Board is fully departmentalized, having the following departments:

>Department of Church Schools
>Department of Education
>Department of Evangelism

Department of Home Missions
Department of Pensions and Benevolence
Department of Publication
Department of World Missions
Department of Youth

Paragraphs 336-68 of the *Manual* describe the duties of these departments.

Lay participation is a distinctive of Nazarene church government from the local to the general church. A careful lay-ministerial balance is maintained throughout the church. For every minister elected to the General Assembly, there is a layman elected. The ratio is one to one. Laymen outnumber ministers five to one at the district assembly. On the local church level, the ratio is one minister to a congregation. This is a church for the layman!

ORGANIZATIONAL STRUCTURE OF THE CHURCH

GENERAL ASSEMBLY

General Superintendents   General Board

DEPARTMENTS OF THE GENERAL BOARD

Ch. Sch. Educ. Evan. H.M. W.M. Pub. P. & B. Youth

DISTRICT ASSEMBLY

Dist. Supt.   Dist. Adv. Bd.   Dist. Officers

LOCAL CHURCH (CONGREGATION)

Pastor

Church Board

| Stewards | Trustees | Education Com.* |
| Sunday School | NYPS | NWMS |

*Local church may choose to have an education committee as part of the church board rather than having a separate church school board.

Principle of Lay Participation In Church Government

General Assembly

Minister — Layman

District Assembly

Ministers — Laymen

Local Church

Minister

Congregation of laymen

For Your Consideration

1. Why do we describe our church as being Wesleyan in doctrine?
2. What are some of the terms used interchangeably for *holiness*? Which term do you personally prefer?
3. Why are Nazarenes described as an evangelistic people?
4. What place does singing have in our holiness tradition?
5. How do you explain the generosity of our people?
6. Explain briefly the basic type of government in the Church of the Nazarene.

Chapter 4

A Church in the Making

No attempt will be made here to give a complete history of the Church of the Nazarene. In the limited space, that would be impossible. Furthermore, it would not be germane to this study. The official history of the denomination is *Called unto Holiness*, by Timothy L. Smith. Another source book for historical background reading is M. E. Redford's *The Rise of the Church of the Nazarene*. Both books may be purchased from the Nazarene Publishing House.

You will want to get acquainted with the story of the church's beginning days. Some of the men and groups so prominent in this exciting story should be familiar to you. A proper appreciation of one's heritage comes only through knowledge. It is such an appreciation that the writer hopes will come from a study of this chapter. Tears, sacrifice, prayers, persecution, and hard work were active ingredients in the church's making.

"A tiny mustard seed . . . becomes the largest of plants" (Matt. 13:31-32, LB). That was the way Jesus described the growth of the Church. That can increasingly be said to be an apt description of the growth of the Church of the Nazarene. Certainly, Nazarenes began as a small group. In 1908 there were only 10,414 Nazarenes in the world. Yet in 1971 they surpassed the half-million mark. Surely the leadership of God is clearly visible in the Nazarene story.

The Church's Founder

In all fairness, no one person can or should be rightly credited with founding the Church of the Nazarene. One might quite honestly refer to the Holy Spirit as the church's Founder. Any spiritually discerning person can readily see the impact of the Holy Spirit on this young denomination. A revival of holiness and interest in preaching biblical holiness culminated in a new denomination. It was the miraculous working of the Holy Spirit that ultimately brought 22 groups together, forming what is known as the Church of the Nazarene.

From the beginning, though, the Holy Spirit has always chosen to work through men. There were many through whom He worked in giving the Nazarenes their church. From a purely human side of the story, there must be a founder. That title goes to Phineas Franklin Bresee. Undoubtedly, he would have been more than willing for the title to go to the Holy Spirit. A man of his humility could see that what was done was the work of God through him.

P. F. Bresee was born on December 31, 1838, in Delaware County, New York. He made his first appearance in a log cabin in the little farm town of Franklin. In later years when he realized he did not have a middle name, he took the name of the town of his birth. Much of his early life was

Phineas Franklin Bresee, D.D.
Founder of the Church of the Nazarene

spent working on the farm. Dr. Bresee relates that he was sent to school at the age of three.[1] Unfortunately his formal education did not last very long. Even so, Girvin rates him high intellectually. His five "mental traits" were: "retentive memory, vivid imagination, keen analysis, marked synthetic ability, and the power of analogy."[2]

At the age of 12, he moved with his family to nearby Davenport, N.Y. They farmed for a while, but then his father began operating a general-merchandise store. Young Phineas began working in the store as a clerk. It was during these teen-age years that he was converted. One day in the store, in February, 1856, a Rev. Smith, a Methodist minister, approached him about his soul. That night he went to the preacher's "protracted meeting." He was the first one in that revival to go to the altar. He was not saved, however, until the following Sunday afternoon in a Methodist class meeting.

A few months later he was given an exhorter's license, which he did not bother to use. Because of his timidity he did not want to get before a crowd. He did, however, do a great deal of personal work and led in prayer meetings from time to time. Despite his timidity, Bresee always felt the call to preach. His own testimony is, "I always felt called to preach from the time I was born, or began to know anything."[3] He was surprised that everybody did not know he was called to preach.

Early in 1857, he was moving with his family to Iowa. On the occasion of his leaving he was forced into preaching his first sermon. Upon arrival in Iowa he learned there were few churches or ministers out there. Soon he found himself engaged as a Methodist minister and a member of the conference. In 1860 he took time out from his ministerial duties to return to New York for personal business. His purpose for returning home was to marry Maria E. Hibbard, whom he had known while living in New York. In August, 1861, he was ordained an elder in the Methodist church. He pastored several churches in Iowa. It was while he was preaching his own revival at Chariton that he was sanctified. This experience was to make a marked difference in him as a man and as a minister of the gospel.

With a gift for preaching and a strong evangelistic fervor he was successful in all his pastorates. Bresee was a man of great passion. When he gave the invitation for sinners to come and pray, it was hard for them to resist. There were some rough pastorates, but he always seemed to be able to make them go and grow. His own determination plus the grace of God made him effective. At the early age of 26, he was a presiding elder in the Methodist church.

A failure in a business venture caused him to leave Iowa and move to California. This business was a sideline designed to supplement his earnings as a minister. In the end it bankrupted him. As he put it,

> I felt some degree of embarrassment at the thought of remaining in a country where I was supposed to be wealthy, when, in fact, I was very poor. Hence I deemed it best to transfer to some distant Conference. I formed the firm conviction at that time that I would never more attempt to make money, but would give the remainder of my life, whatever it might be, to the direct preaching of the Word of God.[4]

This he did until his dying day.

In September, 1863, at the age of 45, he found himself in southern California. His first pastorate was at Los Angeles First Methodist Church. He served several churches in southern California and one year was the presiding elder of the Los Angeles District. His revival methods never failed to bring growth. And they never failed to bring opposition. At Pasadena his membership increased from 130 to 700 in a two-year term as pastor. That's a phenomenal growth rate for any church!

Conflict had begun to develop over the doctrine of holiness in southern California. There was particular conflict over the teaching of sinless perfection. Bresee found himself in conflict with the church leaders on the issue and was forced out of his church.

He had always been interested in helping the poor. The opportunity came to minister in a city mission in Los Angeles. He asked the conference to maintain him as a minister in the Methodist church on a supernumerary (or special) relationship while he worked in the mission. This request was denied. After a night in prayer, Dr. Bresee requested a "location," which meant a severance of any official relationship with his church. Although he had begun his ministry at the age of 18 in the Methodist church, after 37 years of service he was now no longer a Methodist minister.

With his new freedom he was off to Peniel Mission in downtown Los Angeles to work with Rev. and Mrs. T. P. Ferguson. He spent a year in the work there. In the summer of 1895 he spent his time in camp meetings and revivals. While he was away, a telegram from the Fergusons indicated his services were no longer needed. Now he found himself "frozen out" of the mission work he so wanted to do.

A week later a group asked him to preach for them in a rented building not far from the Peniel Mission. Announcements were printed and distributed and a group destined to be known as Nazarenes began worshipping with Phineas Bresee as their minister. The break with the Fergusons was, therefore, more instrumental in precipitating a new denomination than the departure from Methodism.

Fortunately Dr. Bresee lived to see the fruit of his labors. He saw a dream unfold as a new holiness denomination began to emerge. "In 1895 he began the work of the Church of the Nazarene with a handful of believers. During the twenty years that intervened between that time and his death, the church of which he was the honored and beloved leader, had become a host of nearly thirty-two thousand."[5] After those 20 productive years in building the denomination's foundations, Dr. P. F. Bresee went to be with the Great Founder of the Church of Jesus Christ. He died November 13, 1915.

The Birth of a Church

No knowledgeable person would ever refer to the Church of the Nazarene as a split-off from the Methodist church. Phineas F. Bresee did not leave the Methodist church to start a new denomination. It was later when frozen out by the Fergusons that he began the work which resulted in a new church. The "seed" for a new church was planted when he accepted the invitation to preach in a rented building on October 6, 1895. The intention of this group was to carry on "evangelistic and city mission work, and the spreading of the doctrine and experience of Christian holiness."[6]

Eighty-six persons gathered on October 20, 1895, to form a new organization. A few days later the charter was completed with 135 members. Before a name was even chosen, they decided their government should be congregational. J. P. Widney, a medical doctor, suggested the name that was finally accepted by the group. It would be the Church of the Nazarene. Jesus was known as a Nazarene and this title symbolized "the toiling, lowly mission of Christ."[7] The church would thus identify with the poor and working classes of people.

Owners of the rented building soon asked the Nazarenes to vacate. Their shouts of victory were considered noisy and distateful to nearby businesses. A tabernacle with a seating capacity of 400 was constructed. Soon more space was needed and the tabernacle was expanded to accommodate 600 people. Further expansion was necessary and the enlarged facility afforded a seating capacity of 800. In the first year Dr. Bresee took in 365 members. No wonder then that Trueblood said, "The religion of the early Nazarenes, whatever else it may have been, was not mild religion."[8] This was an alive, on-the-move group of people.

Revival fires burned continuously at First Church of the Nazarene in Los Angeles. Even tourists came by the old "Glory Barn," as the tabernacle was called, to see what was happening. The flames spread and before long Nazarene congregations were springing up all over southern California. But the growth of this movement was not confined to California. Nazarene beginnings could be cited in neighboring states, throughout the Northwest, and on to the Midwest.

Rules for membership in Nazarene churches were kept to a minimum. Emphasis was given to the fullness of the Holy Spirit. Christians, it was believed, could be trusted to follow the leadership of the Holy Spirit in matters of convictions and standards. They were joyously free and shouts of glory and victory were commonplace. From the earliest days, the Nazarenes recognized two sacraments: the Lord's Supper and baptism.

Fermenting Holiness Revival

By no means was the revival restricted to the Church of the Nazarene. Everywhere, it seemed, people were becoming interested and experiencing holiness of heart. Often this led to their expulsion from old-line churches. Many times Spirit-filled Christians had to choose between their church and the experience of holiness in their hearts. They were informed that they and their professions of entire sanctification had to go! Forced from their own churches, men had no alternative but to start new centers of worship.

They stayed with their original denominations as long as they could. In fact, as John L. Peters has pointed out, holiness associations discouraged what was known as "come-outism." Holiness people were encouraged to stay in their churches and reform them. Many of them were valiantly courageous and loyal as long as they could be. They were often physically expelled from their churches. When one was thus "crushed out," he most often took others with him. Peters comments, "When a holiness association report speaks of those who seem to be driven out of the Methodist Episcopal Church by its opposition to the definite work of holiness, there are grounds for the statement."[9]

Even before Bresee's Church of the Nazarene was conceived, similar things were happening in the Northeast. As early as 1887, the People's Evangelical church came into being. This group developed out of forthright opposition to holiness in other churches. Other groups sprang up in New England, giving birth to the Central Evangelical Association. There were mergers among these groups. The group that continued to predominate and into which others flowed was the Association of Pentecostal Churches of America. This body of believers was later to come into the Church of the Nazarene. Fred Hillary and Howard Hoople were the standout leaders in the holiness movement in the East. The holiness people in the East generally preferred a congregational form of government.

Down South, God was working in holiness revivals in Tennessee. At Milan, Tenn., the New Testament Church of Christ was organized by Rev. R. L. Harris on July 9, 1894. This holiness church was born "because of the strong conviction that Christians should go back to the purity, simplicity and power which characterized the New Testament Church."[10] Their work spread to other states and the holiness message was being heard. Their churches often were born in tent meetings. Women were allowed and even encouraged to preach in the New Testament Church of Christ. After Harris died, his wife carried on the work for many years. These holiness people were characterized as having strong emphasis on the biblical teachings. Whatever their weaknesses may have been, they knew the Bible!

Rev. J. O. McClurkan organized the Pentecostal Alliance in Nashville, Tenn., in 1898. McClurkan was a Cumberland Presbyterian minister. He had experienced entire sanctification and thought the doctrine should be preached more forcefully than it was in most denominations. His group changed their name to Pentecostal Mission in 1901. Interested in social work, they established a rescue home for unfortunate girls in 1907. Evangelism and world missions were their main interests. At one time they had 30 missionaries. They started a school to train their own missionaries. Pentecostal Bible Training School evolved until it is now known as Trevecca Nazarene College. Their church government was somewhat representative.

In Texas, the New Testament Church of Christ and the Independent Holiness church united to form the Holiness Church of Christ. Rev. C. B. Jernigan was the leader in Texas holiness circles. Many years were to pass before they could condone leaving one's own church to start new groups. But, ejected from their churches, they were forced to make a church home for themselves. Those who had been recently converted and sanctified also needed church homes. The New Testament Church of Christ probably tended to be a bit more legalistic concerning "standards" than did holiness people in other parts of the country.

There were others, too! Methodist laymen formed the Laymen's Holiness Association in the Dakotas. In Scotland there was another holiness movement. There, Rev. George Sharpe, formerly a Methodist and then a Congregational preacher, found himself without a church. The opposition was again to the preaching of holiness. Thus was born the Pentecostal Church of Scotland. England spawned two other such groups: the Interfational Holiness Mission and the Calvary Holiness church of Britain. Then there was the Gospel Workers church in Canada. It's a long and exciting story. You should read it more fully for your own benefit in the official church history, *Called unto Holiness*, by Timothy L. Smith.

SEEING A PATTERN

Seldom were these holiness people contentious or factional by nature. They avoided church "splits" and encouraged those who were sanctified to stay in their old-line churches. They were not protestors whose only badge was negativism. Rather, they were proclaimers of a full gospel and were extremely positive in their approach. Even when they were forced out because of their holiness profession, history does not show that they fought the older churches.

Periodicals always appeared when a new group formed. This pattern was the same whether they were inside or outside their former churches. They had a point of view that needed emphasis and a periodical was deemed the way to propagate it. The printed page was another way of spreading the holiness message. Sometimes their papers became a kind of defensive tool. The periodicals responded to false charges and attacks made on holiness and holiness people, but this was only a minor function.

Ministerial and Bible training schools were the trademark of these new groups. Only a glance at history is needed to verify that holiness groups have always seen the value of education. Colleges, universities, academies, and training schools mushroomed. Later years saw some of these merging. Interestingly enough, universities were merged to become colleges! Even the presumptuous names for the schools cannot hide the interest in education. In the early days the main objective of the schools was to train ministers and missionaries.

With all their differences in the various groups, there was one constant—holiness! Not always were they able to agree when the holiness people made contact. There were, for example, differences of opinion as to what form of church government was most desirable. Either desire for or distaste of what had been known in their former churches complicated this problem. There was not unanimity concerning the place of women preachers. Pre- and post-millennialists contended for their respective view on the second coming of Christ. Varying opinions prevailed as to the best stand to take on tobacco and secret orders. But the one cohesive constant was holiness.

God certainly guided through the formative years of the church. Petty differences were flung to the wind in order to unite as holiness people. Adjustments had to be made by all of the groups as they united one with another.

That holiness was a recurring and predominant theme is evidenced by the prominence of the word "Pentecostal" in the groups' names. Their schools often included "Pentecostal" in their names. No interest in what has come to be called *glossolalia* (spaking in tongues) should be inferred from this. Such phenomena were never the stock-in-trade of the holiness groups which came into the Church of the Nazarene. "Pentecost" was simply a reference to the Day of Pentecost and the infilling of the Holy Spirit. Proof of that experience was a pure heart, not speaking in unknown tongues.

Getting Together

Strong desires for merger and unification of holiness forces began to surface. Mergers were really not simple to work out. Geographical separations complicated and made unions more difficult. Differences of convictions about some things aggravated the matter. Ecclesiastical backgrounds and preferences for church government created critical problems which had to be resolved. Some forthrightly opposed union. "Getting together" in unity was a great miracle, as much so as the inception of these various groups. Timothy Smith believes, "The subsequent union of several of these [holiness denominations] to form the Church of the Nazarene was a miracle indeed."[11]

Mergers of lesser moment took place throughout the revival of holiness. The first big major merger was that of the East group with the West. Rev. C. W. Ruth was one of the most instrumental men in accomplishing this feat. Easterners were used to congregational government. They believed a local congregation should retain the right to secede at any time and take their property with them. The West group was episcopal with a stronger interchurch organization. Compromises were made on both sides. At Chicago, Ill., in 1907, the Association of Pentecostal Churches united with the Church of the Nazarene. The newly merged group took the name "Pentecostal Church of the Nazarene."

Representatives from the Holiness Church of Christ in Texas were present at the Chicago meeting. Already they were slightly interested in a merger. Jernigan and his group insisted, however, on some clarification of certain issues. Pre- and post-millenialism could not mix, they said. They wanted a stronger stand on tobacco and secret orders than had been taken by the Pentecostal Church of the Nazarene. With give-and-take on both sides, the differences were ironed out. Jernigan declared that the Texans got everything they requested. But actually it was holiness of heart and life that forged the union. Little issues seemed to fade away in the light of the big issue. The southerners became members of the Pentecostal Church of the Nazarene on October 13, 1908, at Pilot Point, Tex. This date has been taken as the official birth date of the Church of the Nazarene.

Inevitably the question arises as to why this date is more significant than the others in Nazarene history. Timothy Smith has given three reasons for its importance. First, *it signified a broad acceleration of the trend away from independent associations and independent churches toward a fully organized denominational fellowship.* The Pentecostal Church of the Nazarene had become a church. It was now a denomination in its own right.

The Pilot Point meeting is further memorable for its affirmations of the church's unity in essentials and its determination to maintain liberty in all other things. Certainly this was consistent with the founder's desire. Holiness would not be sacrificed to anyone, but some matters could be left to the individual. Thus the church saved herself from becoming a legalistic, pharisaical denomination.

Pilot Point also signified the establishment of the Church of the Nazarene on a national basis.[12] The church was now a national church. There were more differences to be resolved to bring this about than might at first be imagined. Remember how closely this union followed on the heels of the Civil War and you begin to get the picture. But Yankees and Southerners embraced and had a love feast on October 13, 1908! The church was no longer a sectional group; it was a national denomination.

Other accessions followed, but Pilot Point established the church as national in scope. At the General Assembly in 1919 there were memorials from 35 districts requesting that "Pentecostal" be dropped from the church's name. Since that time the church has been known as the Church of the Nazarene. Confusion of the church with "tongues" groups evoked the request for change in name.

Time Line of Church Development

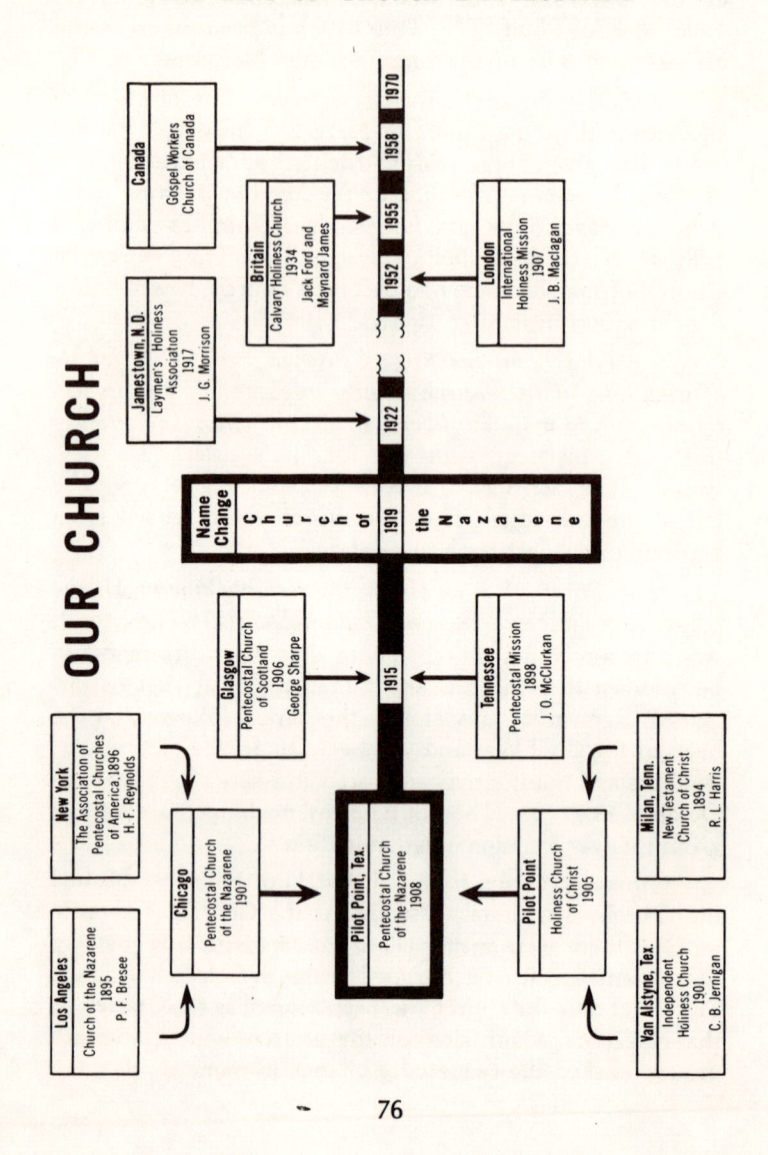

OUR CHURCH

Los Angeles — Church of the Nazarene, 1895, P. F. Bresee

New York — The Association of Pentecostal Churches of America, 1896, H. F. Reynolds

Chicago — Pentecostal Church of the Nazarene, 1907

Glasgow — Pentecostal Church of Scotland, 1906, George Sharpe

Tennessee — Pentecostal Mission, 1898, J. O. McClurkan

Milan, Tenn. — New Testament Church of Christ, 1894, R. L. Harris

Van Alstyne, Tex. — Independent Holiness Church, 1901, C. B. Jernigan

Pilot Point — Holiness Church of Christ, 1905

Pilot Point, Tex. — Pentecostal Church of the Nazarene, 1908

Name Change — Church of the Nazarene, 1919

Jamestown, N.D. — Laymen's Holiness Association, 1917, J. G. Morrison → 1922

Canada — Gospel Workers Church of Canada → 1958

Britain — Calvary Holiness Church, 1934, Jack Ford and Maynard James → 1955

London — International Holiness Mission, 1907, J. B. Maclagan → 1952

1915 — 1970

76

It Has Begun!

Exciting things have happened, but the most wonderful days for the Church of the Nazarene are yet ahead. The church shows no signs of breakdown. Holiness has not been de-emphasized and the evangelistic fervor has not subsided. Nazarenes hope that Trueblood's description of Nazarene religion as "not mild religion" still holds.

Running strongly counter to current church trends, the Church of the Nazarene is still a growing, thriving church. In the past 20 years the church has nearly doubled its membership. In 1973 the year finished with 538,081 Nazarenes in world membership.

While other denominations report steadily declining stewardship, the Church of the Nazarene continues to set new records. Giving for all purposes in 1973 reached a record $117,942,483. Per capita giving was an all-time high of $273.75. Giving for world missions was more than $11,984,921 in 1973. Nazarenes continue to expand their missionary interest while many churches are bringing their missionaries home.

Nazarene colleges continue to grow. Nearly 10,000 students are enrolled in our 11 institutions of higher learning, including 8 liberal arts colleges in the United States, Canadian Nazarene College, Nazarene Theological Seminary, and Nazarene Bible College.

The Sunday schools are growing in the Church of the Nazarene. Sunday school enrollment now exceeds 1 million. Membership in the Nazarene Young People's Society is over 220,000, and in the Nazarene World Missionary Society over 360,000.

You can be proud to be a Nazarene! It is a holiness church with a message that will change lives today. It is a growing church, its impetus for growth being evangelism and outreach. Here is a church—your church—that attempts to grapple with the needs and problems facing men today. In it you can find a place to serve God and the world of our day.

For Your Consideration

1. Who is considered to be the founder of the Church of the Nazarene?

2. Why is October 13, 1908, called the birth date of the Church of the Nazarene?

3. What were the circumstances that led to the formation of the first Church of the Nazarene in Los Angeles, Calif.?

4. What change in name was made in 1919? Why was this change made?

5. Study the chart entitled "Time Line of Church Development" and list the geographical areas from which the groups came who merged to form the Church of the Nazarene.

6. Point out five factors indicative of the continuing growth of the Church of the Nazarene.

Chapter 5

An International Church

Nazarenes may rightly point to their church as a world church. You do not simply belong to a little local congregation. Your church reaches to the four corners of the earth. Wherever you go, you will find your church. There may be a few differences in accents and cultural backgrounds, but they are Nazarenes! Their warmth, sincerity, and friendliness mark them. Evangelistic zeal and a gospel of holiness are their characteristics.

The church will try to keep up with you! When a family moves, it is easy to leave the church and religion in that distant city. Anonymity in the huge metropolitan areas is an ever present temptation. Chances are that someday you too will move from where you now live. Don't get lost and don't wait for the church to find you. You belong to the Church of the Nazarene, International! But in case you do get lost, Nazarenes will try to find you. The Department of Evangelism in Kansas City, Mo., has a service called "Moving Nazarenes." Your pastor writes to Kansas City and they inform the pastor of the church nearest your new home. Contact is made with you, and you are back home in the Church of the Nazarene!

So You're a Member Now

General Superintendent George Coulter has remarked: "It doesn't happen in the Church of the Nazarene until it happens in the local church." How true that is! New Nazarenes are added in the local church. Converts must be won through the local church. Only as the local church pays its budgets is the Church of the Nazarene able to have a district church, general church, or world missions program. It's when money is raised at the local level that we can report the stewardship of the whole church.

That brings us to you! The local church can do only as much as individuals like you do. People just like you make the church what it is. Any criticism leveled against the church is a criticism against ourselves. As the Church of the Nazarene turns out strong, dedicated Nazarenes, she grows in strength. Really, it cannot happen in the local church until it happens with *you*. A record Easter Offering, for example, is received because *you* sacrifice and give. New people are won to Christ and the church because *you* care. Yours is a growing Sunday school and church because of *your* dedicated participation in the church's ministries. Visitors say yours is a friendly church because *you* go out of your way to be friendly. Begin to get the idea? You are important to your church.

What a blessed privilege to belong to the church! There is the fellowship of believers that strengthens you. Now you belong to a church family. You're not a "permanent guest." Whatever happens, you have a voice in the family affairs. In the church this voice gets expressed through the vote. Every member has the right to voice his opinions. And the pastor and church board have an obligation to consider your concerns and suggestions. When asked by the pastor and nominating committee, you are eligible for church offices now. In every way, you are a part of everything your church does.

Church of the Nazarene, *International Headquarters in Kansas City, Mo.*

Privilege is only one side of the coin, though. The other side is obligation. You cannot have one without the other. To say you belong means you must belong to the total program of the church. That means church, Sunday school, NYPS, and NWMS. Nothing in the church program is optional. That is, not if you're a good member. There's the obligation to attend, as you promised, all the services of the church. Attendance at regular services (that includes the midweek prayer service!), special and revival services is assumed. No, it is not mandatory. But why miss any of the blessings God has for you?

Supporting the church is your obligation too. Tithing is not a requirement for church membership. We believe, however, that it is the biblical method for supporting the church. How could anything be fairer than the tithe? You earn $50.00 and your tithe is $5.00. You earn $500 and your tithe is $50.00. As long as you tithe, you are giving proportionately the same as anyone else even though the actual amount may vary. You do not withhold your tithe when you disagree with the pastor and church board! The tithe belongs to God and it is not your right to hold out on God.

Promises should be kept! That applies to the promises to abide by the rules and standards of the church. No one will stand over you and force you to do anything. This must come from inner self-discipline. Your own integrity, as well as that of your church, is at stake. Be a good Nazarene; you are the most powerful advertisement the church has. Make it positive, not negative!

Through your church there will be many opportunities of blessing for you and your family. Religious instruction is one of those opportunities. This you may receive in a number of ways. The sermon, Sunday school class, and NYPS offer potential for instruction. It is only as we gain more knowledge of Christ and His way that we are able to grow in grace. There will be Christian Service Training classes to bring you further instruction on churchmanship, the Bible, and holiness.

You have the opportunity of expressing your Christian faith positively. Witnessing and personal evangelism provide you with means for doing this. Classes on personal evangelism are sometimes offered in the church. Not only are others helped through your efforts, but you find yourself growing stronger in the Lord.

Training opportunities abound in the church. Christian Service Training classes are planned to help you learn how to live the Christian life and to render effective service. Through our CST office in Kansas City, there is a course available for almost everything you want to study. Courses on the Bible, churchmanship, church history, and many other areas are available. Classes may be scheduled in your church so that a group may study together. If this is not practical for you, there is the home study route. Right in your home you can study and earn CST credits! Talk with your pastor or write the CST office in Kansas City about these training opportunities.

Undoubtedly the greatest opportunity your church can give you as a Christian is that of service. Surely you need worship and fellowship. But how selfish to see how much we can get from the church without giving anything in return! Get involved in some phase of service in your church. What can you do? Well, ask your pastor, Sunday school superintendent, NYPS president, or NWMS president. Teaching, helping with the music, visitation—there are all kinds of opportunities for the person who wants to get involved. It may be that the choir director needs your help.

Don't be afraid to do what you feel you can do. Harold Cape isn't! He does not feel qualified to teach and disclaims any ability for music. Many things don't fit into what he feels he can do. You wouldn't find him anxious to get before a crowd. Work schedule forbids serving on the church board. Harold Cape is a handyman! Every year he does hundreds of dollars' worth of repairs on his church and parsonage. No appointment was ever made by the board! No, but he watches carefully for the things that need to be done. Then with speed and skill he does them! Without reluctance he'll tell you this is what God wants him to do.

THERE ARE BUDGETS

No, they are not taxes! It is a way for every member of the church to be involved in the church's program of world evangelism. Through this means the ministry of any local church is enlarged. Just imagine, your church is helping to support missionaries around the world. Your local church helps pay the salaries of our general superintendents. Alabaster money from your church helps build homes, hospitals, and churches on our mission fields. Because you and your church care on a local basis, we have a church with a worldwide ministry. Seen in this way, budgets become a glorious privilege! It is another way of sharing in something that is big—really big!

As is commonly supposed, budgets are not figured on the basis of membership. Each district has its own formula for figuring budgets. They are usually calculated on a percentage basis of money raised in the local church for the church year preceding the district assembly. A copy of the ways and means committee report in the *District Journal* will explain the percentages for the budgets on your district. Ask your pastor to see a copy of the *District Journal.* Informed church members should know these things.

Should we be sending all that money away from the local church? That all depends on how you look at it. It's a matter of your vision! To hoard and keep everything for ourselves is selfish. Such an attitude would reveal shortsightedness, lack of vision, lack of compassion, and a short-circuited religion. No doubt every local church could use all of its money locally. But such a church would become ingrown and selfish. It would become less than a Christian church. Christians are taught to tithe, to share. Then why shouldn't the church share its income too? God will bless the local church that makes an effort to share in the denomination's worldwide obligations.

So what is *the General Budget?* Contrary to common belief, it is not just a missionary budget, although by far the largest block of the General Budget (80 percent) is allocated to world evangelism. This is apportioned in the ratio of 80 percent to 20 percent between the Department of World Missions and the Department of Home Missions. Almost 50 percent of the latter's budget goes to overseas home missions projects. Each of the remaining departments of the general church, except the Department of Publication and the Department of Pensions and Benevolence, derives at least part of its operating funds from the General Budget. A small portion of the General Budget is used for the operation of our denominational headquarters for the International Church of the Nazarene in Kansas City, Mo. Salaries for the general superintendents, executives, their assistants, and office secretaries come from the General Budget. Grants for the operation of Nazarene Theological Seminary and Nazarene Bible College are included in this 20 percent as well. Because the bulk of it is used for world missionary work, much of the General Budget is raised through the Easter and Thanksgiving offerings.

Since the district church organization has expenses, there is also a *District Budget.* The district parsonage and office must be maintained. There are such things as office equipment and supplies (and postage!) that requires expenditures. The district superintendent's salary and travel expenses are paid out of the district budget. Smaller remunerations are paid to the editor of the district newspaper, district secretary, and district treasurer. This is also the way to finance the travel and other expenses of the district advisory board. General Assembly delegates' expenses are paid from the district budget.

Then there's the *Home Missions Budget.* Since 1911 the responsibility for home missions evangelism has been delegated to the districts, even though some financial aid comes from the general church. All the money paid to the home missions budget by your church stays on your district to do the work of home missions. The general church is doing all it can to encourage home missions work on the districts. With approval, interested persons may give toward district home mission projects now and have it counted as a "10 percent special" to be applied on the General Budget. This is the lifeline for starting new Nazarene churches on your district.

Add to your list the *Educational Budget.* Money raised for this budget goes for the support of the Nazarene college on your educational zone. Mounting educational costs make this support imperative. Even with this help, the church college has a struggle competing with state institutions. Without the educational budget, the Nazarene institutions of higher learning could not exist.

And don't forget the *Pensions and Benevolence Budget!* This fund is important to the minister. This is the only way to insure retirement benefits for him and his wife or his widow. Even so, retirement benefits are extremely low for ministers. From this budget, funds are used to pay the premiums for a $1,000 insurance policy for all active Nazarene ministers. When the churches on your district pay 90 percent of their P. & B. budgets, that insurance policy is increased to $2,000. Where deemed necessary, emergency relief is granted to ministers in times of sickness or death.

Never think of your budgets as taxation. Enlarge your

Supports the missionary work

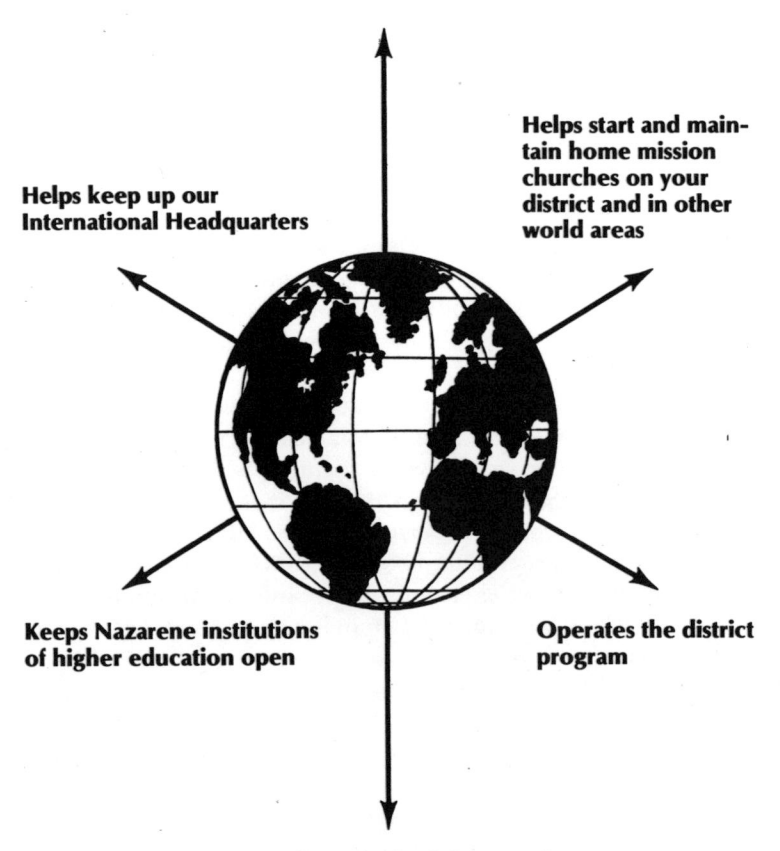

Helps keep up our International Headquarters

Helps start and maintain home mission churches on your district and in other world areas

Keeps Nazarene institutions of higher education open

Operates the district program

Cares for retired ministers and their wives or widows

Look What Your Budget Money Does!
It Makes a "World Church" a Reality.

vision. Try to realize that you belong to a growing world church. In a small way each individual has the unique privilege of being involved in something bigger than he could do alone. The local church can have a share in doing things too big for it to do alone. Teamwork is the key! And you, friend, are part of the team!

A Family of Churches

In the local church, you belong to a family of believers. On the district level, your church is a member of a family of churches. So the family and the fellowship have enlarging borders! The base of Christian fellowship broadens. Opportunities for service multiply as you become a part of the family of churches.

By all means you should attend the district assembly and other district functions. You need to know the other people on the district. Get acquainted with your district leaders. Become involved in the activities of your district. The churches on your district are bound by something stronger than geographical boundaries! In a sense, it is your local church enlarged. There are opportunities through your district that even your local church cannot give you.

Get acquainted with your district superintendent! He supervises the work of all the churches on your district. From time to time he will visit your church and perhaps will preach. There will be times when he comes to promote the work of the district. This man is your pastor's pastor and prays for him and the success of his work. Always he is looking for new places to start home mission churches. When your church needs him, he will come to you. If your pastor resigns, he'll help you find a new pastor. While you are without a pastor, he technically becomes your interim pastor. So, in this big family, you are never left stranded!

Your district probably provides your children and youth with summer camps. These are staffed by pastors and laymen who really care. More and more districts are also sponsoring young adult retreats. What premium can be placed on such values? Yet these are things most local churches could not provide. When the combined efforts of individuals and churches are pooled, many things can be done that otherwise would be impossible. The fellowship and inspiration of district assemblies, conventions, and other gatherings are not to be minimized.

There are service projects that you can participate in on your district. IMPACT teams give youth a wonderful outlet for their faith. In turn they become a part of the district's outreach program. They can often open doors for new work on the district. Youth and adults can help with work projects on the district. Perhaps there is a struggling home mission church. A workday might be called and folk from across the district will come and help paint, repair, landscape—and do whatever else needs to be done. All this because we are a family of churches!

Enlarging Fellowship

Perhaps you come from a relatively small Church of the Nazarene. Quite possibly yours is the only Nazarene church in your community. Sometimes you get a "church inferiority complex." But really, that is not necessary! You belong to something worthwhile and it really is not as small as you sometimes feel it is. Take a good look at what kind of church the Church of the Nazarene is!

You belong to a church which has:

- Over 500,000 in world membership
- 600 missionaries serving the church and God in 50 world areas
  - 7,000 ordained ministers and 2,500 licensed ministers
  - 5,000 churches at home and on world mission fields plus 1,500 preaching points and outstations on world mission fields

- An International Headquarters for this world church located in Kansas City, Mo.
- A publishing house also located in Kansas City, Mo., which is one of the top 10 denominational publishing houses in the world in production volume
- Holds number one place in denominations of 200,000 and more for its per capita giving ($273.75 in 1973)
- Eight liberal arts colleges, a Bible school, and a graduate seminary in the United States, a college in Canada, and Bible schools in Europe, South Africa, and Australia
- Worldwide properties valued at over $500 million
- Over $100 million raised for all purposes each year
- 5,000 Sunday schools and an additional 250 branch Sunday schools, with a total enrollment of 1 million.
- An international radio program of gospel music and preaching called "Showers of Blessing," and a Spanish-language broadcast, "La Hora Nazarena," each of which is aired on approximately 700 stations each week. A Portuguese broadcast was launched in 1972 and one in French in 1974.

A Missionary-minded Church

To keep up interest in and knowledge of the church's world missions outreach, we have the Nazarene World Missionary Society. And that's why we have monthly missionary meetings. From its inception, the Church of the Nazarene has been actively interested in missions. World evangelization has been the burning desire of the church. And now you are part of that missionary endeavor!

So that's why your church takes all those offerings! There is giving through Prayer and Self-denial. Formerly known as the Prayer and Fasting league, its members were asked to pray, and fast one meal a week. The price of the meal fasted was to be given for world missions. In 1972 the name was changed to Prayer and Self-denial, so that other phases of self-denial in addition to fasting might be included. Says Dr. Mary Scott, executive secretary of the NWMS, "It is hoped that the challenge of a real self-denial offering each week, rather than just the price of a meal, will greatly increase the amount given for world evangelism." Then, too, there are Alabaster offerings. Twice each year these offerings are received. Usually they are taken in September and February. Money received through the Alabaster offerings is used to construct buildings on the missions fields. Churches, clinics, hospitals, infirmaries, and missionary homes are built this way. No other funds are allocated for buildings on the world mission fields.

Two major offerings are received each year for missions. Nazarenes around the world are asked to sacrifice in these two offerings for world evangelism. They are taken on Easter and Thanksgiving Sundays each year. All of these offerings—Prayer and Self-denial, Thanksgiving and Easter —are directly applied to your General Budget. Alabaster offerings, although they do not count toward the General Budget, are credited on the church's 10% giving for World Evangelism.

But don't get the idea that the missionary arm of the church is concerned only with money! Finances are necessary, but the primary objective of world missions is souls! There is no other motive that would justify the large expenditure of money each year. Bringing the lost of the world to Jesus is the only reason we have a world missions program.

Missionary work in the Church of the Nazarene is of three main types: preaching, teaching, healing. So the great need is for ministers, teachers, doctors, and nurses. But there is other work. Printers, carpenters, radio technicians, and many others are needed to carry on all the phases of the world missionary program.

A tithing church? Yes, every pastor wants a congregation made up of faithful tithers. In the Church of the Nazarene that principle is taken one step further! Every local congregation as a body should be a tithing church. Ten percent giving for world missions is thought of as the normal. Many churches go well beyond that in giving for world evangelism. Repeatedly churches that are tithing their income for world missions have witnessed the blessings of God. It is in forgetting ourselves and reaching out to others that we can do something for God. Hoarding everything for ourselves causes any church to stagnate and die eventually.

Your Publishing House

Your church's publishing house is the largest printer of holiness literature in the world. Whatever you need to operate the local program of your church, you will likely find it at the Nazarene Publishing House, Kansas City, Mo. The publishing house is not financed or in any way subsidized through the General Budget. Still it has been able to provide first-quality materials to the churches at competitive prices. The chief aim of the publishing house is not to make money, but it funnels back into the general church program many thousands of dollars every year. Its great motivation is to spread the gospel through the printed page.

Books, books, and more books—650,000 a year—continue to roll from its presses. Devotional books, theological books, commentaries, biblical studies, sermons, and practical helps for ministers and other church workers are printed. Then there are Bibles, booklets, pamphlets, and the missionary reading books. Each book, booklet, pamphlet, or tract must be approved by the book committee before it can be printed.

Your church's Sunday school literature is printed at the Nazarene Publishing House. The writing and editing of the material are handled through the Department of Church

Schools. The writers and editors are all Nazarenes dedicated to their church and its doctrinal positions. When the writing of the manuscripts is finished, the publishing house takes over. There are now 52 periodicals published for the Department of Church Schools. In order to provide these materials to you when you need them, they must be printed a number of months in advance. Nazarenes are grateful for a church that will provide its instructional materials for its Bible classes in the church.

Materials and supplies for the NYPS and NWMS are provided through the publishing house. Everything from program outlines for Sunday evening to quiz materials is part of the church's printing task. Record books, study aids, charts, and promotional materials for your NWMS are prepared by your denomination's publishing house. If you need it, chances are it has already been printed!

A number of major periodicals are provided for your reading pleasure and benefit. These publications bring to Nazarene readers the kind of information and resources they need to have. Of course, many besides Nazarenes read these periodicals.

The *Herald of Holiness* is a biweekly magazine. Every Nazarene home is encouraged to subscribe. Annually a subscription campaign is held in the local churches. The *Herald* is a colorful and attractive periodical. Informative and inspirational literature is packed into every issue. Articles are geared to the needs of people. Feature articles and the editorial page are standard fare. Beyond that, the articles vary in content and message.

Edited and prepared by the Department of World Missions, the *Other Sheep* is the official world missions voice of the church. Subscriptions are received in the local church through a campaign sponsored by the Nazarene World Missionary Society. The magazine is a monthly publication. Stories of the work on the mission fields form the bulk of the material. A consistent reading of the *Other Sheep* would help a church member to be informed about Nazarene world missions. Through its pages Nazarenes at home get better acquainted with their missionaries and the world mission fields.

Conquest is the church's monthly magazine for teen-agers. It is beamed toward high school readers. Its articles are often written by the young people themselves. Every issue tries to deal with the real problems confronting today's Christian youth. Subscribers are enlisted in the local church by the NYPS's annual subscription campaign. Because of its high-quality material, every youth should have *Conquest* in his hands.

ETC. is a monthly magazine prepared for the post-highs, college youth, and young adults. Its articles are beamed to the interest and needs of the above-mentioned target audience. It is tabloid size, attractive in format, and relevant in its message.

Come Ye Apart is a devotional quarterly based on the Home Daily Bible Readings of the adult Sunday school curriculum. Its large circulation testifies to its contribution to the spiritual well-being of our people.

These periodicals are not printed just for sales. Every Christian home needs good literature to read. The materials are prepared with the aim of helping readers develop as Christians. "As he thinketh in his heart, so is he" (Prov. 23:7). Really, a person becomes what he reads. The church has accepted the responsibility of providing the right kind of materials for its membership to read.

Materials prepared by the Nazarene Publishing House are sold under three different imprint names. When a book is expected to be sold primarily to Nazarene readers, it will bear the imprint, "Nazarene Publishing House." Other books that are expected to have a wider circulation bear the imprint "Beacon Hill Press of Kansas City." Often this difference in imprint name breaks down barriers so that good Nazarene materials get into other than Nazarene hands—and minds! Music is published under the "Lillenas Publishing Company" imprint. Many denominations other than the Church of the Nazarene regularly use "Lillenas" music. All of these materials are printed at the same place—your Nazarene Publishing House!

World Headquarters

The International Headquarters for the Church of the Nazarene are located at 6401 the Paseo, Kansas City, Mo. While not luxurious or extravagant, Nazarene Headquarters is impressive. You can rightly be proud of your church's International Headquarters. Visitors are always welcomed and, if they desire, are given guided tours through the offices. A tour service in Kansas City regularly brings tourists by to see Nazarene headquarters.

At the International Center there are four attractive buildings. The main Headquarters Building has a fitting symbol for an international headquarters—a world globe revolving continuously atop its central tower. This globe symbolizes the worldwide mission of the church. The General Board Building houses editorial offices for the Latin publications, *Herald of Holiness*, Christian Service Training, Department of Evangelism, Department of Youth, Department of Church Schools, and the Department of Education. Here also are the General Board Auditorium and committee rooms. Nearby is the Nazarene Book Store. Its customers are by no means limited to members of the Church of the Nazarene. At the south end of the 22-acre property is the Nazarene Theological Seminary.

The offices for the general superintendents are located in the International Headquarters Building. Business takes them out of town most of the time, but Kansas City is home base for them. Efficient secretaries keep the offices operating while the church's leaders are away. From these offices the work of the six general superintendents reaches out to the remote areas of the world.

The General Board has a room set aside for its meetings in the General Board Building. Annually members of this 40-member board with the general superintendents, the general secretary, and general treasurer meet here. During the year, employees of the International Headquarters use the General Board room as a chapel.

Employees of your church's headquarters do not forget that their work is spiritual in nature. At 9 a.m. every day a bell rings. This signals all employees to stop for a brief prayer period. Machines are turned off and work ceases as heads are bowed in prayer. When special needs arise in the church or with individual employees, prayer requests are given over the intercommunication system.

All departments of the General Board have offices at the International Center with the exception of the Department of Publication. Its offices are at the Nazarene Publishing House, 2923 Troost Avenue, in Kansas City. Any questions you may have about any of these departments or their services may be directed to the respective department at 6401 The Paseo, Kansas City, Mo. 64131.

International? Yes, the church is international in scope. Wherever Nazarenes are, they think of Kansas City as their world headquarters. It is to Kansas City that they look for direction and guidance. Promotional materials and ideas come to the local churches from Kansas City. More than this, the church is not merely a local organization. Its responsibilities are to the world. Its message is for the whole world. Nazarenes may well join with John Wesley in saying, "The world is . . . [our] parish!"

Educational Institutions

Attempting to give the historical background of our educational institutions would serve no purpose here, even if space would allow. You should be aware of these institutions and know where they are located, particularly the college on your own zone. Inquiries about these schools should be directed to the respective institutions.

All of them are committed to the beliefs and standards of the Church of the Nazarene. The same standards apply to the campuses as apply in the local churches. Each of the colleges has a godly and well-qualified faculty. Young people in the local churches should be encouraged to enroll in Nazarene colleges. Here they will receive quality education in a spiritual atmosphere.

A roll call of the Nazarene educational institutions goes like this:

Bethany Nazarene College
Bethany, Okla. 73008

British Isles Nazarene College
Manchester, M20 8GU, England

Canadian Nazarene College
Winnipeg 19, Manitoba, Canada

Eastern Nazarene College
Quincy, Mass. 02170

Mid-America Nazarene College
Olathe, Kans. 66061

Mount Vernon Nazarene College
Mount Vernon, Ohio 43050

Nazarene Bible College
Colorado Springs, Colo. 80901

Nazarene Theological Seminary
Kansas City, Mo. 64131

Northwest Nazarene College
Nampa, Idaho 83651

Olivet Nazarene College
Kankakee, Ill. 60901

Pasadena College
Pasadena, Calif. 91104

Trevecca Nazarene College
Nashville, Tenn. 37210

From the earliest days the Church of the Nazarene has been committed to education. As soon as churches were started, schools were also organized. That commitment still holds. There is ample justification for the Nazarene colleges today. When you are able to see what they are doing, paying the educational budget to the college on your zone becomes a sheer delight.

For Your Consideration

1. How does the church seek to keep up with moving Nazarenes?

2. List some of the benefits and obligations of membership in the church.

3. In your own words explain the purpose of the various budgets.

4. What are the two major offerings received each year for missions?

5. In what ways does the Nazarene Publishing House serve the church?

6. Where are the International Headquarters of the Church of the Nazarene located? Name the four main buildings at the International Center.

Chapter 6

Beliefs and Standards

"It doesn't matter what you believe as long as you are sincere!" That cliché sounds good, but it expresses a falsehood. Sincerity does not validate a doctrine. A father may sincerely give his child poison, thinking it is medicine. But the child may die just the same! What you believe does matter greatly. A doctrinal position is justified only when it is the clear teaching of the Bible.

You have heard it said, "No creed but Christ for us!" But any explanation of that "creed" reveals there is more. Creeds and dogmas will not save anyone, but every Christian needs to know what he believes and why. God is not at all displeased when He has intelligent Christians on His hands! Christians should be able to discuss and substantiate with scripture what they believe. The Church of the Nazarene does have a creed. Every Nazarene has an obligation to be familiar with and understand that creed.

THE NAZARENE CREED

What we believe is of utmost importance. Beliefs have a direct bearing on behavior. Nazarenes have never believed an elaborate creed was necessary. The church does not try to tell its membership in minute detail what it must believe about everything. Matters of faith that are considered essential to Christian experience are brief. New members of the church are asked to avow that they believe these statements in the creed before they are received into the Church.

Stated briefly and simply the Nazarene creed follows. We believe:

1. In one God—the Father, Son, and Holy Spirit.
2. That the Bible is God's Word and contains all truth necessary to be saved and live the Christian life.
3. That everyone is born with a fallen nature and is thus inclined to evil.
4. That unless a man repents, he will be eternally lost.
5. That anyone who repents and believes on Jesus Christ will be saved.
6. That Christians are to be sanctified wholly through faith in Jesus Christ.
7. That when a person is saved or sanctified the Holy Spirit witnesses to him, assuring him the work is done.
8. That Jesus Christ is coming again.

Tolerance is encouraged in beliefs in other matters. The church has never tried to say what millennial theory one must hold concerning the Second Coming. But in these eight creedal statements unanimity is desired. One who does not honestly feel he can subscribe to these simple statements of belief should most likely seek another church home. Most Christians would not find it difficult to endorse this brief creed.

The Articles of Faith

Fifteen articles of faith have been adopted by the Church of the Nazarene. These become an expression of the church's theological stance. Historically they date back to the 39 articles of the Anglican church. Descending from

Anglicanism, Methodism adopted 26 articles of faith. From these the Church of the Nazarene derived its 15 articles of faith. They serve as a kind of definition of the church's "minimum theology."[1]

It will be helpful to study this chapter with the Bible in one hand and the church *Manual* in the other. An explanation of what is meant and a scriptural foundation for each of the articles will be attempted here.

I. *The Triune God*

The Trinity certainly was never intended as a mathematical enigma. It was not designed to puzzle Christians. Yet few thinking men will boast a thorough understanding of the doctrine. Jesus, however, commanded the Church to baptize "in the name of the Father, and of the Son, and of the Holy Ghost" (Matt. 28:19). In John 15—17, the Son prays to the Father and asks that the Holy Spirit be given to the disciples. In Luke 24, He talks of returning to the Father but promises the Holy Spirit will come.

The concept of the Trinity (triunity), while not entirely clear, is not entirely foreign to human personality either. As an individual this writer is a "three-in-one" person. To his daughter he is father and she calls him "Daddy." His wife knows him as husband and calls him "Darling." There is a congregation that thinks of him as their minister and calls him "Pastor." Why then should we quibble about the Holy Trinity being totally inexplicable?

II. *Jesus Christ*

Jesus, born in a lowly stable, was the promised Messiah. He was born of a virgin, Mary (Matt. 1:18; Luke 1:27; Isa. 14:7). Conception was by the Holy Spirit and not man (Matt. 1:18; Luke 1:35). This conception was miraculous. No biological explanation (i.e., parthenogenesis) is adequate. As He himself claimed, He was the Son of God (Luke 1:35).

Thoroughly human, He could hunger, thirst, grow weary, and be tempted. Yet He was so divine He could say, "Thy sins be forgiven thee" (Luke 5:20). He is God (John 10:30). He laid down His life for sinners, and as He promised, on the third day arose. It is His death that gives us salvation.

III. *The Holy Spirit*

Jesus recognized the person of the Holy Spirit when He said, "When He [the Holy Spirit] is come" (John 16:13). He teaches, guides, and speaks. Conviction for sin is His unique work (John 16:8-9). A person may be possessed by and be filled with the Holy Spirit. John said Jesus would baptize with the Holy Ghost [Spirit] (Matt. 3:11). Paul admonishes us to be "filled with the Spirit" (Eph. 5:18). The prophecy in Joel 2:28 was fulfilled on the Day of Pentecost (Acts 2:13). It is the Holy Spirit who sanctifies the believer (Acts 15:8-9).

IV. *The Holy Scriptures*

Nazarenes take the Bible seriously. From Genesis to Revelation it is the Word of God. Good and godly men wrote the Bible under the inspiration of the Holy Spirit. "All scripture is given by inspiration of God" (II Tim. 3:16). It is the rule of life for the Christian. It is not a book of rules, but is a Guidebook to life for those who will seriously consider it.

Inspiration was not mechanical nor were the personalities of the writers negated. The Holy Spirit inspired, directed, guided, and superintended the writing of the Bible. Nazarenes believe in "plenary inspiration." That is, the Bible is fully inspired in every part (John 10:35). It is a divine-human Book. God inspired it and men wrote it down. This is not without human parallel. A businessman tells his secretary to write a letter and gives the essence of the message. She writes the letter and he signs it. Legally his signature makes it his letter. In some sense at least this is how the Bible is God's Word.

V. *Original Sin, or Depravity*

The "fall of man" dates back to Eden (Genesis 3). Through Adam sin passed on all men (Rom. 5:12). By nature, the whole human family is depraved. All men are not as bad as they might be, but none in his own moral goodness is good enough. Every man can testify with David, "Behold, I was shapen in iniquity, and in sin did my mother conceive me" (Ps. 51:5). All men need the saving grace of God. None by his own effort can earn God's salvation. "For by grace are ye saved through faith; and that not of yourselves" (Eph. 2:8).

VI. *The Atonement*

God's holiness cannot abide sin. Sin separated man from God (Genesis 3). But Jesus came to save men (Luke 19:10). Atonement could be made for man's sin only by His blood (Rom. 5:9). He came to be "a ransom for many" (Mark 10:45). "For if, when we were enemies, we were reconciled to God by the death of his Son, much more, being reconciled, we shall be saved by his life" (Rom. 5:10).

Central to the Christian story is the cross of Christ. With a cross, God bridged the gap between man and himself. Through His cross and blood "we have peace" with Him (Rom. 5:1). Atonement has been made. "For he is our peace, who hath made both one, and hath broken down the middle wall of partition between us . . . that he might reconcile both unto God in one body by the cross" (Eph. 2:14-16).

VII. *Free Agency*

No robot he—man is really free. Adam and Eve were created holy but with the power of moral choice. They deliberately chose sin. By His own self-limitation, not even God can force holiness and righteousness on anyone. Constantly we are reminded: "Choose you this day whom ye will serve" (Josh. 24:15; Matt. 6:24).

By giving man the power of choice, God could create only moral possibilities. The possibility of holiness meant also the possibility of sin. But Jesus is the Light and that Light "shines upon every man" (John 1:9, Phillips). God's grace appears to all men (Titus 2:11). Everyone receives his opportunity; thus individuals become responsible for their choices. You are free to choose but you cannot determine the consequences of your choice. Whatever you sow, you reap (Gal. 6:7).

VIII. *Repentance*

"For godly sorrow worketh repentance to salvation" (II Cor. 7:10). It is the Holy Spirit who brings such "godly sorrow" and conviction for sin (John 16:8). Some make the mistake of seeing this godly sorrow as itself being repentance. Such is not the case. It only sets the stage for true repentance.

True repentance is possible only where there is an understanding of the nature of sin. "Sin, when it is finished, bringeth forth death" (Jas. 1:15). Sin is no light, laughing matter. It is serious and requires repentance. True repentance requires a thorough change of mind and a turning away from sin. To the woman caught in the act of adultery Jesus said, "Go, and sin no more" (John 8:11). There is no repentance without a change of character (Matt. 3:8). Repentance was the basis of the preaching of John the Baptist (Matt. 3:2) and of our Lord (Matt. 4:17).

IX. *Conversion*

Conversion is a broad and general term. It encompasses justification, regeneration, and adoption. These are separate acts of God but take place simultaneously; together they are known as conversion. Jesus can change one's life. We are justified by faith (Rom. 5:1). Release from the guilt of sin allows us to testify with Paul, "There is therefore now no condemnation to them which are in Christ Jesus" (Rom. 8:1).

Christ gives life to those "dead in trespasses and sins" (Eph. 2:1). By His regenerating power, we pass "from death unto life" (I John 3:14). His power renders each of us a "new creature in Christ Jesus" (II Cor. 5:17). Then we are adopted as children of God (Rom. 8:15). To each He gives His witness that we are "the children of God" (Rom. 8:16). Conversion takes place when one turns his back on sin, finds divine forgiveness, and follows Christ.

X. *Entire Sanctification*

Sanctification becomes a necessary second work of grace because of the dual nature of sin. Sin is not only an *act*; it is a *disposition*. This truth is verified throughout the Scriptures. In the Ten Commandments, not only is stealing forbidden, but also covetousness (Exod. 20:15, 17). David prayed for forgiveness and for cleansing (Ps. 51:1, 10). Jesus goes behind the *act of adultery* to the *disposition to adultery*, and forbids both (Matt. 5:27-28).

John came preaching a baptism of water repentance that anticipated a baptism by fire (Matt. 3:11). Jesus prayed for His disciples to receive the Holy Spirit and to be sanctified (John 15—17). This prayer was answered on the Day of Pentecost (Acts 2). He told His disciples that they would be filled with the Holy Spirit (Luke 24:49; Acts 1:8). Sanctification and the baptism with the Holy Spirit are the same experience (Acts 15:8-9). Paul exhorted Christians to be sanctified wholly (I Thess. 5:23).

XI. *The Second Coming of Christ*

Probably none of the articles of faith have more relevance for our day than this one. Jesus clearly taught that He would come again (Matthew 24; Mark 13). Paul's second letter to the Thessalonians concerns itself with this subject. Peter was explicit about it (II Peter 3). Said Jesus, "If I go

. . . I will come again" (John 14:3). Even as He went away, an angel announced that He would come again (Acts 1:11).

Date setting is for the curious; preparedness is for the wise. Jesus said that no one, including himself, knew when He would return (Mark 13:32). The certainty that He would return prompted the timely admonition to "watch" (Matt. 13:37). The parable of the 10 virgins (Matthew 25) underscores the need to be prepared for His coming at all times. Nazarenes are an expectant people. They are looking for their Lord to come again. All the signs point to His soon return. In this "blessed hope" they labor and wait (Titus 2:13).

XII. *Resurrection, Judgment, and Destiny*

Nazarenes believe in the resurrection of the body. The best that can be said on the resurrection has already been said (I Corinthians 15). God not only will redeem our souls, but we wait also for the "redemption of our body" (Rom. 8:23).

All will be resurrected (I Thess. 4:16), some to life and some to death. After the resurrection, there will be a judgment day (Heb. 9:27). Judgment will be according to the deeds done in the body whether they be good or evil (II Cor. 5:10). To those on His right He will say, "Come, ye blessed of my Father, inherit the kingdom prepared for you from the foundation of the world" (Matt. 25:34). But those who have ignored Him will hear these words: "Depart from me, ye cursed, into everlasting fire, prepared for the devil and his angels" (Matt. 25:41). There is no reprieve or appeal from this judgment.

XIII. *Baptism*

"Repent, and be baptized" (Acts 2:38), is the New Testament formula. An Ethiopian eunuch (Acts 8:36) and a Philippian jailer (Acts 16:33) found that to be the formula. Baptism is important; it is a New Testament command, not to be taken lightly. John the Baptist came baptizing and so did the disciples of Jesus (John 4:1-2). Jesus' Great Commission involves baptism as well as witnessing (Matt. 28:19). Baptism is an outward sign of an inward state of grace.

Nazarenes believe in infant baptism. There is ample historical, theological, and biblical justification for this. Parents who present their infants for baptism are asked to give assurance that the child will be given Christian training. The *Manual* provides that those who do not prefer to have their children baptized "but simply dedicated or consecrated" may do so.

The mode of baptism is strictly the choice of the applicant. There is no clear New Testament teaching of any specific mode. It may be administered by sprinkling, pouring, or immersion. If one transfers to the Church of the Nazarene from another denomination, he need not be baptized again.

XIV. *The Lord's Supper*

On the eve of His death, Jesus initiated this sacrament. That it was to be a continuing sacrament is evidenced by His command, "This do in remembrance of me" (Luke 22:19). Jesus said, "This cup is the new testament in my blood: this do ye, as oft as ye drink it, in remembrance of me" (I Cor. 11:25). First Corinthians, chapter 11, gives the most detailed account of the New Testament view of the Lord's Supper. True, it is a memorial, but Christ is present in a real way at His table. For Nazarenes the Lord's Supper symbolizes His death, resurrection, and second coming (I Cor. 11:26). Pastors are required by the *Manual* to serve Communion to their congregations at least quarterly.

XV. *Divine Healing*

Much of the Lord's earthly ministry was taken up with a ministry of healing. Why then should anyone doubt either His ability or willingness to heal? Elders of the church are to be called when one is sick. They are to lay hands on the ill person and pray for his healing, and "the prayer of faith shall save the sick" (Jas. 5:15). As much as Nazarenes believe in divine healing, there are no commercial "faith healers" in the denomination's ministry. They do not find the use of medicine, doctors, and hospitals inconsistent with a vigorous faith in divine healing.

STANDARDS OF CONDUCT

High standards of ethical conduct have long marked the Nazarenes. Nor is this a day to suggest lowering them. As Christians, we ever need the warning not to let the world squeeze us "into its own mold" (Rom. 12:2, Phillips). In the Crimean War a young officer got to the top of a hill and set the colors there. It seemed impossible for the regiment to make it to the ridge and the cry arose, "Bring the colors down!" The officer shouted back: "No! Bring the men up to the colors!"[2] And so we cry today, "Bring the men up to the standards!"

From earliest days Nazarenes have refused to have a legalistic code of conduct. Rules have been kept to a minimum. They believe that sanctified people can be trusted to the leadership of the Holy Spirit. Holiness of heart takes care of Christian ethics. As Peter put it, you are to "be holy in every department of your lives" (I Pet. 1:16, Phillips). Yet there is the need for some guidelines for conduct. Our leaders feel that "the ethical standards of our church are well expressed in the General and Special Rules. They should be followed carefully and conscientiously as guides and helps to holy living."[3]

No attempt was ever made in the *Manual* of the Church of the Nazarene to give a complete list of "do's and don'ts" for Christians. Such a list is not only impossible, but also impractical. Principles are needed and they have been given in the *Manual*. They are reasonable and scriptural. "Those who violate the conscience of the church do so at their own peril and to the hurt of the witness and fellowship of the church."[4]

Standards often imply negativism. Some church members, it is feared, know more about their church's prohibitive rules than about its creed. A balanced approach has been taken by Nazarenes. There are positive as well as negative standards—seven of each! Both are important. Following the positive standards of the church will make the negative ones fairly easy.

I. *Negative Standards*

The principle is simple: "Avoiding evil of every kind." The seven prohibitions are but illustrations of the principle. They serve to clarify and define what is "evil." It's an old principle. Paul stated it: "Abstain from all appearance of evil" (I Thess. 5:22). This is a worthy goal toward which to strive and one toward which every Christian will gladly work.

1. *Taking God's Name in Vain*[5]

Profanity is such an inexcusable sin that it hardly seems necessary to mention it. Apparently, though, the necessity always existed, for it is forbidden in the Ten Commandments. God saw it as a serious offense, for "the Lord will not hold him guiltless that taketh his name in vain" (Exod. 20:7). Again the command was given, "Neither shalt thou profane the name of thy God" (Lev. 19:12). James pleads that "above all things, my brethren, swear not" (Jas. 5:12). Even for non-Christians, profanity is in the poorest of taste. To say the least, the use of such language reveals a limited vocabulary.

2. *Profaning the Lord's Day*

This prohibition, like the first, comes directly from the Ten Commandments (Exod. 20:8-11). When He worked six days and rested on the seventh, God set the pattern. Jesus underscored the importance of this commandment by declaring himself to be "Lord also of the sabbath" (Mark 2:28). That the Lord's Day has replaced the Jewish Sabbath does not void the commandment. It should be said that Christ's resurrection, not an edict of Constantine's, changed the day for worship from Saturday to Sunday. The Lord's Day should be a happy and joyful day. It should be reverenced by avoiding unnecessary business and labor. Physically as well as spiritually, a man needs a day of rest. The soul needs a chance to catch up with the body!

3. *Tobacco and Alcohol*

Science now says what the church said for some time about alcohol and tobacco. Alcoholism is America's number one drug problem. The use of tobacco has been directly related to cancer. So it's a matter of the stewardship of our bodies. As far as alcohol is concerned, Nazarenes insist on total abstinence. Social drinking is taboo. What other stand could the church take when 25,000 people die on American highways in alcohol-related accidents every year? The use of tobacco is forbidden, not to be hard on folks, but to remind them of their responsibility to God. "Know ye not that ye are the temple of God, and that the Spirit of God dwelleth in you? If any man defile the temple of God, him shall God destroy; for the temple of God is holy, which temple ye are" (I Cor. 3:16-17).

4. *Quarreling, Gossiping, and Slandering*

Quarreling, gossip, and slander are wrong because such use of the tongue is unlike Christ. To gossip and slander is mean and beneath the dignity of a Christian. Paul said it well: "Let all bitterness, and wrath, and anger, and clamour, and evil speaking, be put away from you, with all malice: and be ye kind one to another, tenderhearted, forgiving one another, even as God for Christ's sake hath forgiven you" (Eph. 4:31-32). "They must not speak evil of anyone, nor quarrel, but be gentle and truly courteous to all" (Titus 3:2, LB). "Don't repay evil for evil. Don't snap back at those who say unkind things about you" (I Pet. 3:9, LB), is the way Peter put it. It takes two persons to quarrel, and the Christian is responsible to see that it doesn't happen! Jas. 3:5-18 reminds us that the undisciplined use of the tongue is dangerous and damaging.

5. *Dishonesty*

Transparent honesty is demanded in the Sermon on the Mount (Matt. 5:33-37). One's life and speech should be consistently honest. Fraud in business is wrong. Questionable practices in business should be avoided (I Cor. 6:7-10). "Let us walk honestly, as in the day" (Rom. 13:13). Or as *The Living Bible* puts it, "Be decent and true in everything you do." The Ten Commandments forbid lying (Exod. 20:16).

6. *Pride in Dress or Behavior*

Solomon told us long ago that "pride goeth before destruction" (Prov. 16:18). Whatever its form of expression, pride is deadly to the spiritual life. "A man s pride shall bring him low" (Prov. 29:23). "God resisteth the proud, but giveth grace unto the humble" (Jas. 4:6). Modesty and simplicity, becoming to holiness, is the New Testament standard (I Tim. 2:9-10). Adornment is to be of "the hidden man of the heart" rather than external decoration (I Pet. 3:3-4). In all fairness, it should be said that simplicity and modesty as principles in dress apply to men as well as women. Immodesty in dress is not only unchristian; it is in the poorest of taste.

7. *Ungodly Entertainment*

Any form of entertainment "not to the glory of God" does not merit enjoyment by Nazarenes. Unless it makes you a better person or a better Christian, there is a question as to whether one should involve himself in such an activity. "Know ye not that the friendship of the world is enmity with God? whosoever therefore will be a friend of the world is the enemy of God" (Jas. 4:4). Regardless of what we do, Christians should "do all to the glory of God" (I Cor. 10:31). Love for the world is inconsistent with love for God (I John 2:15-16). All "looseness and impropriety of conduct," whether in entertainment or otherwise, is out. Nazarenes are to avoid membership in oath-bound secret orders or fraternities.

II. Positive Christian Action

Life is made up of negatives and positives. The Church of the Nazarene recognizes this and challenges its membership with both negative and positive standards. Not only are they "against" some things; they are just as much "for" some other things. A life that exemplifies the beauties of the positive standards will have little trouble with the negative ones!

1. *Courtesy to All Men*

How important it is for Christians to be courteous! For Nazarenes who make so much of perfect love, they are reminded that love "is not arrogant or rude" (I Cor. 13:5, RSV). Put plainer, Phillips translates this statement, "Love has manners." The Sermon on the Mount deals largely with respect for human personality. Basically, that is what is meant by Christian courtesy. Gentleness or courtesy is one of the fruits of the Spirit (Gal. 5:22). Kindness, love, and courtesy are Christlike virtues (Titus 3:2; Eph. 4:32; I John 3:18).

2. *Financial Support of the Church*

Tithing is in the bargain! Malachi insisted on tithing and said to withhold the tithe is the same as robbery (Mal. 3:8, 10). Jesus supported the idea of the tithe (Matt. 23:23). Paul established the tithes-and-offerings way as the financial plan for the Church (I Cor. 16:2). However, the phrase "as God has prospered him" puts a great load of responsibility on some. That may mean that some should go far beyond the tithe. Really, tithing is "minimum giving" for Christians, and the liberal heart usually does more in response to the love and grace of God. Drudgery and reluctance have no place in giving, "for God loveth a cheerful giver" (II Cor. 9:7). Real stewardship does not begin with the pocketbook, but with the heart.

3. Being Helpful and Charitable

When a brother has a burden, the Christian helps him bear it (Gal. 6:2). Paul reminds us that this is true "especially unto them who are of the household of faith" (Gal. 6:10). The Church is a family—and brothers and sisters look after each other. Hospitality among Christians makes good sense. Nothing is more needed by most Christians than a lot of wholesome fellowship with others of like faith. The Christian, of course, seeks to be helpful and kind to all men.

4. Complete Love for God

Questioning Jesus, a young lawyer asked what the greatest commandment might be. He was trying to trap Jesus, but Jesus gave a forthright answer. Love God with your whole being—that's what Jesus said (Matt. 22:36-40). He had already said it—"Seek ye first the kingdom of God, and his righteousness" (Matt. 6:33). The Great Commandment of Jesus was harking back to the Shema of the Jewish Torah—Deut. 6:5. What a goal for Christians to strive toward!

5. Church Attendance and Devotions

In the Early Church there seems to have been the clear recognition of regular times of worship (Acts 2:42). The writer of the Hebrews urges that Christians not forget to assemble for worship (Heb. 10:25). Instruction in God's Word and the Christian way of life is invaluable (II Tim.

2:15; 3:14-17). "As newborn babes, desire the sincere milk of the word, that ye may grow thereby" (I Pet. 2:2). Group worship is needed, but so are family devotions (Deut. 6:6-7) and private times of prayer (Matt. 6:6). Private and public worship combine to make us growing, sturdy Christians. When the pastor urges regular church attendance, it's not just for the statistical chart! It's because he knows God's Word requires it—and that you need it!

6. *Helping Others*

Nazarenes see the social implications of the gospel. They seek "to do good to the bodies and souls of men." That includes food baskets for the hungry, clothing for the naked. It means visitation of the sick and imprisoned, the fatherless and widows (Jas. 1:27). At the judgment, Christ will consider these matters. Those who have helped the needy will be told, "As ye have done it unto one of the least of these my brethren, ye have done it unto me" (Matt. 25:40). Those will be told to enter into heaven (Matt. 25:35-36). Condemnation awaits those who have failed in this regard (Matt. 25:41-43). "If someone who is supposed to be a Christian has money enough to live well, and sees his brother in need, and won't help him—how can God's love be within *him*?" (I John 3:17, LB)

7. *Witnessing and Soul Winning*

A holiness church is to be active in witnessing and soul winning. To be a non-witnessing holiness church would be a contradiction. A Spirit-filled Christian who does not try to win others for Christ is also a contradiction. That's what being filled with the Spirit is all about (Acts 1:8). Paul was willing to do everything to win the lost. Summing it up, he says, "I am made all things to all men, that I might by all means save some" (I Cor. 9:22). "We are now Christ's ambassadors, as though God were appealing direct to you through us. As his personal representative we say, 'Make your peace with God'" (II Cor. 5:20, Phillips).

III. Cooperative Standards

Unity was necessary for the Holy Spirit's coming on the Day of Pentecost (Acts 2). Such unity must be maintained if the Church is to function in a way pleasing to God. This truth Paul emphasized in writing to the churches at Corinth (II Cor. 13:11), Philippi (Phil. 1:27), and Ephesus (Eph. 4:3-6). Peter also encouraged unity and oneness in the Church (I Pet. 3:8).

Vows are made to be kept. Your church vows are just as sacred as your marriage vows. To break one or the other has serious consequences. Since you voluntarily joined the church, you should never do anything to hurt or hinder it. When you cannot support it fully and wholeheartedly, you probably should seek another church home. This is not to imply that we must all see "eye to eye." It does mean that loyalty to the church, its doctrines and strictures is important.

The following editorial appeared in the *Herald of Holiness*, September 29, 1971, and is reprinted here because it sums up well what a healthy attitude toward church rules is.

On Drawing the Line

Forty years ago a mother wrote to Dr. J. B. Chapman, then editor of the *Herald of Holiness*:

"I am a mother who is trying earnestly to guide my children in the right way," she said. "But there are so many questions about things the children can do and can't do that I am often at my wit's end. Can't you give us a list of things that our children, especially our children in the public schools, can do? They complain that we just want them to sit around and twiddle their thumbs."

Dr. Chapman's answer is classic. Justice cannot be done to it without quoting it in full. He combines the law and the spirit of the General Rules of the church so beautifully. The advice given then is just as pertinent and relevant today. It gives the spiritual, non-legalistic approach of the church to Christian ethics.

"I do not think I could give you a list that would be dependable or useful. Conditions vary in different communities.

"But I think in the interest of the positive and the practical that parents should be careful about drawing lines and forbidding too many things. You can bring on a 'conscience' about things that otherwise might have remained innocent and you can become guilty of just what your children accuse you of.

"I had a neighbor who listened to the impractical people about him and forbade his children's playing croquet and just about every other game, and forbade their taking part in just about everything that appealed to them.

"The result was that home became a bore to the children and 'society' held an appeal like 'stolen waters' that was abnormal.

"When my neighbor was a grandfather, he said to me one day, 'If I had it to do over I would be different. I don't care what the impractical people say, I would make home enjoyable to my children and I would just draw the line on what is actually wicked, not on the innocent things that have no moral character unless you ascribe one to them.'

"But the sad part is that neighbor had lost his children to Christ and the church and he thinks it is because he made the Christian life appear to be both barren and impractical.

"I think just about the worst possible attitude for parents is that which holds that everything adults have lost desire for is wrong for children and the young, and that 'When the young find salvation they will lose their love for these things too.' And in the meantime they compel their children to be abnormal either by enforcing rules which have no meaning to the young or making outlaws of their children by condemning what they do and yet suffering them to do it.

"I would say, make the list of prohibitions as short as possible, and make it on the line of what is actually wicked. As to the rest, trust for a spiritual rather than a legalistic solution, and you will save your children many temptations to outlawry and hypocrisy, and in the end they will most likely turn out to be good citizens and worthy Christians."

This, then, is the Church of the Nazarene. It is a church with a glowing history; God's hand has been evident all the way. It is a holiness church in the Wesleyan tradition. As a denomination she stands in the mainstream of Protestantism. She has a creed; her doctrines are explicit. The high standards of the church are not intended to be a legalistic code, but guidelines for conduct. By both creed and conduct she seeks to be a witness to our day!

For Your Consideration

1. Why is it important for Christians to understand clearly what they believe?

2. How many Articles of Faith are listed in the *Manual* of the Church of the Nazarene?

3. In your own words explain our position on the inspiration of the Scriptures.

4. What is our belief regarding baptism?

5. List the seven negatives in our special rules. List the seven positive challenges.

6. Why is loyalty to the doctrines and standards of the church important?

Reference Notes

Chapter 1:

1. H. Orton Wiley, *Christian Theology* (Kansas City: Beacon Hill Press, 1952), II, 476.

Chapter 2:

1. Elton Trueblood, *The Company of the Committed* (New York: Harper and Row, 1961), p. 21.
2. Elton Trueblood, *The Incendiary Fellowship* (New York: Harper and Row, 1967), p. 15.
3. *Ibid.*, p. 22.
4. Samuel M. Shoemaker, *With the Holy Spirit and with Fire* (New York: Harper and Row, 1960), p. 67.
5. Wiley, *op. cit.*, III, 107.

Chapter 3:

1. Timothy L. Smith, *Called unto Holiness* (Kansas City: Nazarene Publishing House, 1962), p. 113.
2. *Ibid.*, p. 115.
3. William Jensen Reynolds, *A Survey of Christian Hymnody* (San Francisco: Holt, Rhinehart and Winston, Inc. 1963), p. 17.
4. Edward Dickinson, *Music in the History of the Western Church* (New York: Charles Scribner's Sons, 1908), p. 255.
5. Leslie Parrott, *Introducing the Nazarenes* (Kansas City: Nazarene Publishing House, 1970), p. 32.
6. *Knight's Treasury of Illustrations* (Grand Rapids, Mich.: William B. Eerdmans Publishing Co., 1963), p. 49.

Chapter 4:

1. E. A. Girvin, *Phineas F. Bresee: A Prince in Israel* (Kansas City: Nazarene Publishing House, 1916), p. 24.
2. *Ibid.*, p. 19.
3. *Ibid.*, p. 28.
4. *Ibid.*, p. 72.
5. *Ibid.*, p. 20.
6. M. E. Redford, *The Rise of the Church of the Nazarene* (Kansas City: Nazarene Publishing House, 1948), p. 47.

7. Smith, *op. cit.*, p. 111.
8. Trueblood, *The Incendiary Fellowship*, p. 31.
9. John L. Peters, *Christian Perfection and American Methodism* (New York: Abingdon Press, 1956), p. 142.
10. Redford, *op. cit.*, p. 114.
11. Smith, *op. cit.*, p. 205.
12. *Ibid.*, pp. 221-22.

CHAPTER 6:
1. Harold W. Reed, *You and Your Church* (Kansas City: Beacon Hill Press of Kansas City, 1967), pp. 57-58.
2. Richard S. Taylor, *Preaching Holiness Today* (Kansas City: Beacon Hill Press of Kansas City, 1968), p. 23.
3. *Manual, Church of the Nazarene, 1972* (Kansas City: Nazarene Publishing House, 1972), p. 5.
4. *Ibid.*
5. Much help was received in giving biblical bases for the General Rules from W. T. Purkiser's pamphlet *The Bible and the General Rules* (Kansas City: Nazarene Publishing House, n.d.).